THE JULES VERNE COMPANION

THE JULES VERNE COMPANION

PETER HAINING

Designed by Christopher Scott

BARONET
PUBLISHING COMPANY

NEW YORK

Dedicated to the memory of
I. O. EVANS
who fired so many enthusiasms for
Jules Verne – including my own

'If I can speak with any authority
for many other inventors and research workers –
and numerous conversations
convince me that I can – then there is no doubt
that the author of the *Extraordinary Voyages* must be ranked
amongst the most powerful artisans of that scientific
and industrial evolution which is one of the
characteristic features of our age.'
French scientist Georges Claude, 1965

THE JULES VERNE COMPANION
First Baronet Printing October 1979
Copyright © 1978 by Peter Haining
and Pictorial Presentations

First published 1978 by Souvenir
Press Ltd.

ISBN: 0-89437-071-5

Baronet Publishing Company
509 Madison Avenue
New York, NY 10022

CONTENTS

JULES VERNE

ROBUR - LE - CONQUÉRANT

DESSIN PAR L. BENETT

J. HETZEL ÉDITEUR

THE MASTER OF PROPHECY

by Peter Haining

Jules Verne stood at literary cross-roads, between the romanticism of yesterday and the realism of tomorrow. From his genius stem the science fictions of today.'
Victor Cohen, *The Contemporary Review 1956*

Jules Verne was born in 1828 when the scientific age had scarcely dawned, yet when he died in 1905, the emerging Twentieth Century promised an era when man was poised to unlock the great secrets of his own world and explore the possibilities of others in the universe beyond. While he was no technician, nor indeed scientist, Verne had played a very real part in this amazing burst of progress achieved in less than a century: for he was an inspired dreamer, a prophet who 'saw' and wrote about what lay in store for mankind long before it happened.

Verne's primary achievement was undoubtedly to give expression to many of the scientific and romantic aspirations of his contemporaries: he took what might at first sight seem like impossibilities and by the most careful application of existing knowledge and reasoned guess work gave the reading public a foretaste of the future. Nor did he stop at that as Kenneth Allott, one of his first biographers tells us in *Jules Verne* (1940): 'Verne stimulated beliefs in progress, science and industrialism, while he provided an escape from the impersonality and squalor that seemed inevitably associated with the industrial age.'

Perhaps, though, above all else, he was a visionary who saw with his inner eye scenes which he described with such remarkable accuracy and in such a way that his millions of readers saw them just as clearly, too. And in the 65 volumes which made up his remarkable œuvre, *Les Voyages Extraordinaires* there is, as the critic J. W. Lambert has remarked, 'hardly a spot on, under or above the earth which he did not vividly describe, hardly a development in practical science, at least in his earlier years, which he did not press into service with an imaginative vitality which threw off forecast after correct forecast of the shape of things to come.'

In a nutshell, Jules Verne gave the world Science Fiction. Admittedly the 'wonder' story had been in existence long before his time; what he did was to take the ideas which were currently beyond the scope of scientific achievement, yet were a part of man's dreams, treat them seriously and exploit them systematically. He combined information with an exciting yarn: dealing always with *probable* things. As Norman Mackenzie put it most concisely in an article about the Frenchman in *The New Statesman* in September 1956, 'He fused the adven-

Bayard's famous illustration of the splashdown in *From the Earth to the Moon* (1865). (*Facing page*) Title-page of the first French edition of *Robur le Conquérant* (1886) which became *Clipper of the Clouds* in English.

was science fiction, for on closer examination we can see that all writers of adventure stories also owe him a very real debt of gratitude. For he was the first to introduce into his narratives the contemporary achievements of science or engineering, and thereby creating what the Verne authority, I. O. Evans has categorised as 'technical fiction' — 'the type of literature in which Nevil Shute for one excelled.'

If, indeed, we go through the 65 volumes of *Strange Journeys* we find that they can be divided into four specific groups: terrestrial, aerial, aquatic and ingenious. And, taken as a whole, it is easy to understand how Verne so captivated his audience and why Kenneth Allott, for instance, sees him as a modern Scheherazade, 'No sooner did the reader put down one book than another was coming from the presses to take him willy-nilly up the Amazon, or round the Solar System, or anywhere else equally improbable and exciting.'

Yet, having said all this, what sort of a person was Jules Verne? What sort of life did this man of such remarkable imagination and prophetic genius live? The facts are surprisingly mundane.

The son of a Nantes lawyer, Jules Verne passed an unexceptional childhood and undistinguished schooling with only the suggestion that he might have begun developing his imaginative powers because of unconfirmed stories that he drew pictures of strange ships and flying machines in his exercise books. His sole 'adventure' was an attempt to run away to sea which was frustrated by his father before the ship had left the coast of France. Following a sound thrashing he delivered the judgement which virtually summed up the rest of his life, 'After this I shall travel only in my imagination.'

In 1848 he went to Paris to study for the law and also began his literary career by writing several plays and *libretti* for the theatre. A few of these were performed, but earned him little attention and even less money, and in despair he turned to stockbroking. While working on the Paris bourse, a chance sight of a leaflet describing a proposed tour around the world which was being organised by the English travel agent, Thomas Cook, changed his life. This, and his meeting with Jules Hetzel, the Parisian book and magazine publisher who was to become his life-long editor, publisher and friend.

The first story which Hetzel accepted from Verne was *Five Weeks in a Balloon* in 1864, and Kenneth Allott vividly constructs that crucial moment in the young writer's life:

The ill-fated *Great Eastern* which featured in *A Floating City* (1871) and prophesied the modern 'soap opera' — also a group of passengers watching the mysterious 'woman in black'.

ture stories of Scott and Fennimore Cooper with the neo-necromancy of Poe, and by setting this new formula in the frame of modern technology he accomplished the transition from magic-fiction to science-fiction.' And Mr Mackenzie adds, 'To write about four million words of this stuff without a ghost, and to do the reading that his books required, is no mean achievement.'

Yet, it would be wrong to think that Verne's only contribution to literature

Verne started to thank him, but Hetzel interrupted him in the middle of a phrase and began talking of his magazine. All Jules Verne's reserve melted. He attacked Hetzel with his ideas for a series of novels on science and exploration. As he talked his embryonic scheme developed and became a living reality to him. 'Sit down quietly', said Hetzel, and, when Jules stopped striding and did so, he added: 'Now tell me again all your plans'. So Jules took a long breath and spoke of desert islands, trips on rafts up the Amazon, journeys beneath the sea, voyages to the centre of the earth and round the solar system, attempts at conquering the poles, adventures among tattooed or blubber-eating peoples. Hetzel listened. He was listening to a summary of the 'Extraordinary Journeys' which he and his son would publish, year after year, as they all grew older and the appearance of life changed with an ever-increasing rapidity.

The success which Verne and his publisher went on to enjoy is now legendary and as it will be traced through the pages of this book in both words and pictures needs no repeating here. Hetzel, for his part, had no doubt as to why his latest author was destined for immortality:

'The novels of Jules Verne have come just at the right time. When an eager public can be seen flocking to attend lectures given at a thousand different places in France, and when our newspapers carry reports of the proceedings of the Academy of Sciences alongside articles dealing with the arts and the theatre, it is surely time for us to realise that the idea of art for art's sake no longer meets the needs of the time we live in, and that the day has come when science must take its rightful place in literature. To M. Jules Verne goes the merit of being the first to tread this new ground . . .'

But fame and fortune brought no dramatic change in Verne's lifestyle: he retreated to a big house in Amiens and there dedicated himself to work until the end of his days. His one extravagance was a steam yacht which he sailed occasionally on the Mediterranean until ill-health stopped

(*Top*) The power-mad despot, Ker Kerraje, possessor of an 'atom bomb' in *For the Flag* (1896).
(*Bottom*) The mammoth cannon with which the sinister German Professor Schultz threatens to bombard his opponents in *The Begum's Fortune* (1879).

him; and his only personal voyaging was a single trip each to Britain and America and two brief visits to Scandinavia. Almost the entire store of his enormous knowledge which he poured into his books was based on painstaking research and assiduous reading of the latest newspapers and magazines. Towards the end of his life the huge collection of cuttings and articles on which he drew filled an entire room in his home.

It was against this unexceptional, even suburban background that Verne began to issue his remarkable world-shaking forecasts which later played such a significant part in scientific developments. And in time men of action and scientists around the world were singing his praises: Berget in his oceanographic laboratory in Paris expressed his debt to Verne's undersea explorations; Belin, inventor of the Belinograph which resulted in television said Verne had shown him the way; and Rear Admiral Byrd flying to the Pole wrote, 'It is Jules Verne who led me there'. Simon Lake noted in *Submarines in War and Peace* how he had followed the example of Verne's *Nautilus*, and arctic explorers and adventurers like Nansen, Philippe d'Orleans, Brazza and Marchand similarly paid homage to the lead he had given them. (In more recent times the names of Santos Dumont, Marconi, Norman Casteret and Yuri Gagarin are just a few more on the ever-expanding list of people who were inspired by the 'Strange Journeys'.) Yet for his part, Verne remained a modest and unassuming soul throughout his life: 'All that I imagined,' he once remarked, 'will remain below the truth, for a time will come when the creations of science will surpass those of the imagination.'

Today, as we mark the 150th Anniversary of Verne's birth and look over the range of his books, we can see how many of his prophecies have come true and I believe that it is worth mentioning them here both as a record and in the hope that the reader might feel inclined to turn the original pages once more. For simplicity, I have surveyed the books in chronological order.

In one of his very earliest works, *From the Earth to the Moon* (1865) he is off to a remarkable start almost literally anticipating, from blast-off to splash down, the stages of a moon flight as it now actually happens. Verne, we know, left as little to chance as possible in his tale (as he did with many others) by having his cousin, Henri Garcet, a cosmographer and

mathematician, check all his calculations. He could not have realised, of course, that the idea of firing the moon shell from a gun was quite impractical – the projectile and its occupants would have been crushed to atoms when the gun was fired – but this apart, the prophecies are staggering. For instance, he places the launching site as Tampa Town, Florida, which is on almost exactly the same latitude as Cape Canaveral. The shell is made of the right kind of metal, aluminium, and its weight and height are correct in relation to the proposed trajectories. The parameters it follows are accurate, and he anticipates the very necessary system of air regeneration for the crew, and realises the only way the vessel's course can be changed is by rockets. He also forsaw the experimental use of animals before human space flight was attempted, and his telescope sited on the Rocky Mountains differs only by inches in magnifying power and a few miles in location from the giant instrument now located on Mount Palomar.

From the Earth to the Moon was such a success with the public that numbers of people actually believed

Verne had flown to the planet and applied to go with him on his next voyage! Among these were several women who made it quite clear they were offering the author more than just companionship. Verne dismissed such approaches contemptuously, 'What, play Adam to some daughter of Eve up there? No, thank you! I should be meeting a selenite serpent next!' What he did do, though, was set to and write a sequel, *Round the Moon* (1870) which though it added little to the technical prophecies of the first, did advance the idea of a satellite orbiting the planet.

In *Twenty Thousand Leagues Under the Sea* (1870) Verne devised Captain Nemo's remarkable submarine, and although it would be wrong to claim for him the invention of such underwater craft, he was the first to see their true possibilities. At the time he wrote the story experiments were already taking place in France, and the American, Robert Fulton, who built the first practicable submarine, honoured Verne by naming the vessel, the *Nautilus*. (Verne's *Nautilus* is actually two hundred foot long, driven by electrically powered screws, and can be

(*Facing page*) Cover illustration for the French edition of *The Chase of the Golden Meteor* (1908) about a scientist's attempts to draw a solid gold meteor down to earth.

Remarkable illustration from first French edition of *Twenty Thousand Leagues Under The Sea* (1870) featuring Captain Nemo's submarine, the *Nautilus.*

manoeuvred by hydroplanes like horizontal rudders or by filling and emptying her tanks. The crew members also have a special miniature boat with which they explore the sea bed, underwater suits, and even guns which fire electric bullets giving a lethal shock.)

A Floating City which appeared in 1871 was based on the sole transatlantic crossing Verne had made in 1867 from Liverpool to New York and back in the ill-fated giant liner, the *Great Eastern*. This story of the lives and loves of an assorted group of passengers on board the ship has recently been seen by a reviewer in the American science fiction magazine, *Astounding Science Fiction* (December, 1957) as prophecying the modern 'soap opera'! I think I can do no better than quote his words:

'It has a plot that belongs in soap opera and was therefore ahead of its time . . . right out of afternoon TV or radio. Will the dashing Captain MacElwain regain his lost sweetheart? Is the mad woman in black the fair Ellen? Will her husband, the villainous international gambler Drake, force MacElwain into a duel and cut him down? If the captain kills the gambler, how can he ever marry the widow of the man he has slain? Will Ellen ever regain her sanity?'

Not surprisingly, by 1875, Verne had something of a reputation as a prophet of the future, and in December of that year he was invited to give a lecture to his local *Academie* on 'Amiens in the Year 2,000 A.D.'. Because of his interest in the well-being of the town (he served for several years on the Municipal Council) it was not unexpected that behind many of the humorous proposals for his 'Ideal City' were several he hoped to have taken seriously. In his 1973 biography of his grandfather, Jean-Jules Verne gives us a précis of this fascinating address:

'In fantasy, the speaker is astonished to find Amiens transformed overnight into the city that its inhabitants would like it to be: the trains to and from the city are through-corridor trains (requests for which had been ignored by the railway company for years); the thoroughfares are lined with comfortable benches and lighted at night (another bone of contention). Toll charges have been abolished and the muddy streets repaved with cubes of porphyry. Ladies' fashions have reached the supreme heights of refinement (a familiar target for Verne's satire). Marriages have boomed owing to the introduction of a Bachelor Tax — and births have become so numerous that "a five hundred nursepower baby-feeding machine" has had to be

installed. The city has a tram network (another grievance satisfied) and a posh department store; and a telegraph hook-up enables "a Polish pianist in the employ of the Emperor of the Sandwich Islands to be heard simultaneously in London, Vienna, Paris, St. Petersburg and Peking". Because all the doctors in town have adopted Chinese medical techniques and their patients pay only so long as they keep well, hardly anyone falls ill any more. "The music of the future" in the form of a *Reverie in A minor on the Square of the Hypotenuse*, is dispensed by the

Band of the 324th Regiment; it is "neither human nor celestial — no lilt, no beat, no melody, no rhythm: quintessence of Wagner, audio-mathematics, cacophonomania — like an orchestra tuning up" [*Music Concrete*, perhaps]. But from fantasy the speaker is brought back to firm reality by the sight of the mini-geyser spouting once again from the burst main in the middle of the square; as usual the station clock is slow; and the ministerial delegate at the annual Agricultural Show is making his usual boring speech.'

Although Verne was in a light-hearted mood when he gave his address, he was quite serious when he put forward a revolutionary proposal for the working people of Britain, whom he had looked upon as sorely

oppressed ever since his one visit to the country in 1859. The suggestion was made in *Child in the Cavern* (1877) a novel which drew for its inspiration on the Scottish coal mining communities. 'Although unsuited for crop production,' Verne wrote, 'this cavern could have served to house an entire population. Who knows, one day in the constant temperatures of the collieries of Aberfoyle, Newcastle, Alloa and Cardiff, once their deposits have been exhausted, the working classes of England may find their refuge.'

The luxury travelling machine which can move over land and water in *The Steam House* (1880).

Verne's mood was clearly growing more pessimistic and he undoubtedly sensed war in the air when he wrote *The Begum's Fortune* in 1879. This story concerns a sinister German Professor Schultz who has created a mammoth cannon with which he is threatening to bombard all those who oppose him. The man also has at his disposal 'Carbonic Acid Gas' which is not hard to see as a forerunner of chemical warfare. In the opposition which is mounted against Schultz, Verne foresees civil defence measures, fire fighting services and preparations for mass evacuation. But it is with the character of the professor and his unshakable conviction that his countrymen are the master race who must one day rule the world, that the author is clearly most concerned – as I. O. Evans has explained: 'Verne also plainly foresaw grim possibilities in the Teutonic character, and these were only too clearly realised when "German" became almost a synonym for "frightfulness". Though his illustrator Leon Bennett represented Schultz as a moustacheless Bismarck, the character of that sinister personage more foreshadows that of the Nazi warlord, Hitler, his Stahlstadt is a predecessor of the modern totalitarian states, and his published works suggestive of *Mein Kampf.*' It may perhaps be a relief to the reader to known that when Schultz does fire the cannon a serious flaw is revealed – the velocity is so great that the missiles fly beyond the earth's gravity where they immediately become orbiting satellites!

A year later, in 1880, Verne was more his old self when he issued *The Steam House* about the travels of a wonder machine across British India. The story itself is unexceptional, but the machine can be seen as a prediction of the luxury motor caravan, particularly as such means of travel was unknown then, while the nearest equivalent, the traction engine, was cumbersome and slow.

The Clipper of the Clouds (1886) was a much more important work on several counts and shows Verne at the very height of his imaginative powers. In the story he introduces the *Albatross*, a flying machine driven by airscrews which are once again worked by his old favourite, electricity. His main purpose in the book, though, was to underline his conviction that the heavier-than-air vessel would in time prove more successful than the then in favour lighter-than-air dirigible balloon: a belief which, of course, has been triumphantly fulfilled. As far as the craft itself is concerned, a Dr R. C. Pankhurst, of the Aerodynamics Department of the National Physical Laboratory, has commented that although the array of seventy-four small lifting screws which propel the *Albatross* would be much less efficient than just one large screw, the machine does foreshadow certain developments of modern helicopteral practice. Nor does the uniqueness of the story end there: for the material of which the vessel is made has been seen as a form of plastic, while the 'super-accumulators' which drive it might well prove a method of propulsion for aircraft of the future when all the world's oil supplies have been exhausted. Perhaps the most extraordinary claim of

all advanced for this book is that by I. O. Evans who says that the inexplicable aerial phenomena which are introduced at the start of the book can only be described by the modern term 'Flying Saucers'!

It was in 1889 that perhaps the most remarkable of all Verne's stories of prediction appeared – and it is remarkable in that not only had it waited four years to be published, but it appeared in *English* in an *American* magazine! The story is called 'The Day of an American Journalist in 2889' and such is its fascination and rarity that I have reprinted it as the final item in this book. Verne actually wrote the item in

J. T. Maston of the Gun Club who devises the super-explosive to make possible mineral excavation beneath the ice in *The Purchase of the North Pole* (1889). These two pictures are from the first French edition of the work, now among the rarest and most valuable of all Verne titles.

1885 after being approached by Gordon Bennett, the editor of the influential *New York Herald* who asked him to create 'an imaginative account of life in the United States in a thousand years time'.

As we know – and Verne demonstrated the fact in his books – he was fascinated by America and the Americans and saw them as the nation where the most important scientific developments would take place. In his study, *The Political and Social Ideas of Jules Verne* (1971), Jean Chesneaux tells us, 'In the world of the mid-nineteenth century it was the United States which came closest to the "model for development" of which Verne dreamed in the interests of humanity. It provided a perfect setting for his scientific and social forecasts. It inserted itself quite naturally into his project, and it is not by chance that in twenty-three of his novels, out of a total of sixty-four [the one further title in the series was a collection of short stories – Editor's note] the action takes place on American soil, either wholly or in part, or that American characters play an important role.'

Strangely, and for reasons which are still unknown, the story remained in manuscript with Bennett until 1889 when it appeared in a magazine called *The Forum* with which he was also associated. (It has been suggested that Bennett was unhappy with Verne's picture of America as powerful beyond measure and the idea that a descendent of his, Francis Bennett, should, to all intents and purposes, become the uncrowned King of the World – and tried in vain for some time to have changes made.) In any event, the story positively abounds with predictions: there are aerial liners which can travel thousands of miles linking the world; underground railways connect Europe and America; moving pavements save people walking; homes are equipped with combined telephone and television receivers; advertisements are projected on the clouds; news is 'televised' to subscribers as it happens; hibernation and electrically-induced hypnotic sedation are available to the public (a forerunner of cryogenics?) and so on; but I must not spoil all the reader's enjoyment of the story by giving everything away.

Propeller Island which appeared in 1895 is also set in America and concerns a 15 square mile artificial,

One of the huge caves which Verne suggests could be turned into an underground community in *Child of the Cavern* (1877).

propeller-driven island reserved exclusively for millionaires. Naturally the inhabitants are catered for in extreme luxury, and most activities can be performed over the 'teletograph' system without taking a step outdoors. In his description of a piped music system, Verne is clearly prophesying 'muzak' and there is a nice touch in his idea of newspapers printed in chocolate ink on edible paper which can be eaten when they are finished with! It has been suggested that 'Standard Island', as this remarkable creation is called, may have been the inspiration for the 'Mulberry Harbours' which were used so effectively by the Allied Forces in World War II.

An anticipation of the seaplane some twenty years before its invention was Verne's spectacular idea in *Before the Flag* (1896). In a letter to his brother, Paul, at the time he was writing this book, Verne said, "I am trying to find a formula for this vessel. The most original idea would be to have a

ship capable of sailing under the water, on the surface, and in the air as well. But shall I go this far?' In the completed work, the craft becomes the *Ebba* controlled by a ruthless adventurer, Ker Kerraje, who rules the waves like some modern buccaneer. Kerraje also recruits the services of an unbalanced inventor, Thomas Roch, who has developed a chemical explosive capable of pulverising a fleet of ships or a whole city. 'This weapon,' I. O. Evans says, 'so strikingly suggests an atomic bomb that the reader almost needs to be reminded that the book was written before the pioneer work of Becquerel and the Curries paved the way for researches into atomic structure.' Further, the fuse material for this bomb foreshadows the VC's and ICBM's of modern times.

Although Verne's story, *The Hunt for the Golden Meteor* (1908) contains no direct prophecies, it is an interesting piece of science fiction about a scientist who invents a 'neutral helicoidal ray' to attract down to earth a solid gold meteor which has been spotted in the heavens. When the scientist becomes aware of the greed developing all around him among people waiting to pounce on the

meteor, he changes his calculations and deflects it into the sea where it is lost. By a strange piece of coincidence, that same year the book was published, a real meteor crashed with terrible force in the forests of Siberia!

The final works which Jules Verne wrote have with some justification been looked upon as the outpourings of a disillusioned man, for he was growing more and more of the opinion that man's own base nature was demeaning many of the high hopes of science. In *The Barsac Mission* (1914) which was left incomplete on his death and finished by his son, Michel, a tyrant appropriately named Harry Killer wages a war of attrition on the world from his hideout, Blackland, in the Sahara Desert. In his employ he has a scientist who seems to care little about what use his inventions are put to — and among these are a means of controlling the weather, remote controlled guided missiles, and a fleet of variable wing gliders that take off and land vertically, the thrust being provided by engines working on the compressor—burner principle (like turbojets) driving helicopter-style rotors. These 'wasps', as their inventor calls them, are undeniably an early step in

The man who can control thoughts in *Dr. Ox's Experiment* and the evil time-keeper in *Master Zacharius.* (Both 1874.)

the modern science of cybernetics. Another writer, Rupert Gould, says that the book is also 'remarkable for its close anticipation of modern broadcasting' which at that time Marconi was just bringing to fulfilment.

The very last story which Verne wrote was *The Eternal Adam* (*c.* 1905) which he dictated almost on his death bed. It deals with a distant future in which an archaeologist discovers an ancient manuscript describing a global catastrophe in the Twentieth Century brought about by the stupidity of mankind. Only seven people survive this disaster and find themselves faced with the task of painstakingly rebuilding civilisation. In this short tale, Verne's warning to tread carefully along the new paths which science has opened up during his lifetime is clear and unmistakable.

These, then, are some of Jules Verne's prophecies which have come true. There are others which may well be realised with the passage of time as I. O. Evans indicates in this note:

Even some of his minor ideas, which he put forward facetiously, have been shown by his successors as amenable to serious treatment. Dr Ox [in *Dr Ox's Experiment* (1874)] influencing a community's thoughts is suggestive of Big Brother in fiction and Dr Goebbels in real life. Gil Braltar [from the collection, *Hier et Demain* (1910)] leading the apes of 'the Rock' to attack its garrison has been excelled in science fiction by experts training a variety of animals to wage super-scientific warefare. More seriously, the failure of the time-keepers of *Master Zacharius* (1874) is the first example of what in some modern science fiction stories has been called the 'death of metal'.

And, of course, Verne's influence has spilled out into other spheres. As the pages of this book show, there have been films made of quite a number of his stories, and not a few science fiction movies of recent years owe much to him. That greatest of all cinema box office successes, 'Star Wars' began to germinate in writer-director, George Lucas's mind through, he says, his reading of Verne; while those recent popular television series about the Bionic Man and Woman have their antecedents in the previously mentioned experiments of Dr Ox.

The revival of interest in Verne has, of course, now made editions of his books collectors' items where a few years ago they were carelessly handled and casually discarded. (For example, the price in 1977 for a first edition in French of the rarest of his titles, *Sens Dessus Dessous – The Purchase of the North Pole* (1889) – was over £1,000). The illustrated editions in particular are now much sought after, and there is no denying that Verne's success with readers was aided to a considerable degree by the superb artists Hetzel employed, in particular Leon Bennett and George Roux. I have been fortunate in being able to locate many of the best pictures which accompanied Verne's stories, and in the pages of this book the reader will find a representative illustration from every single one of the 65 'Strange Journeys'.

A recent enquiry made by UNESCO has established that Verne is the most translated of all French authors and over the years he has appeared in every major language in the world. No longer is he regarded as a writer of juvenile fiction (an impression that apparently developed because many of his works first appeared in Britain as serials in the *Boy's Own Paper*, which was edited by W. H. G. Kingston, Verne's main English translator) and increasingly his work is being studied and analysed in scientific and technical journals. Indeed, there now seems little disputing that few other writers have matched either his uniquely varied output or the compulsive readability of many of his novels.

And so, finally, if we should look for one single reason to perhaps explain why this reclusive, dedicated, imaginative man should have found immortality, it is perhaps that expressed by his fellow countryman, Jean Chesneaux:

'If Jules Verne and his *Voyages Extraordinaires* are still alive for us, it is because they – and with them the whole of that fascinating nineteeth century – were already posing the problems which the twentieth century has not been, and will not be, able to avoid.'

TWO GLIMPSES OF THE MOON
by George Orwell

In the realms of prophetic fiction, George Orwell's name is nowadays as well-known as that of Jules Verne, although the author of that terrifying view of the future, *Nineteen Eighty-Four* was only born in 1903 when Verne was in his final illness. Orwell enjoyed many of Verne's books in his youth, and in 1941 was called upon to review one of the first — and pehaps still the best — biograpies of the Frenchman. The book, *Jules Verne* by Kenneth Allott obviously intrigued Orwell and his review which appeared in *The New Statesman* of January 18, 1941 pays particular attention to the implications of scientific progress. It should perhaps just be added that Orwell's own two great works of prophecy followed not long afterwards, *Animal Farm* in 1945, and *Nineteen Eighty-Four* in 1949, although his prediction in this essay that 'it seems doubtful whether Verne will be read much longer' has fallen rather short of the mark!

Like most writers, Jules Verne was one of those people to whom nothing ever happens. At an early age he made an attempt to run away to sea, only to be ignominiously recaptured after a few hours, and this was, one might say, his last adventure until late in his life a young man with a fancied grievance shot at and wounded him with a revolver. In 1848 Verne tried to visit Paris during the street fighting, but failed to get there because all the trains were full of National Guards. In this incident one can see the justification for Hitler's remark that ability to write marks a man out as unfitted for a life of action. And this and much else in Mr Allott's book brings out the fact that writers resemble one another much more closely in their private lives than in their writings. Behind the most diverse books there is nearly always the same background, the nerve-racked, dun-haunted figure of the professional writer, paddling about in a dressing-gown in a room full of stale fag-ends and half-empty cups of tea, and struggling with a dreadful book that never gets any further. It seems strange that so unliterary a writer as Verne should have behind him the familiar history of a nineteenth-century Frenchman of letters. But it is all there — the early tragedies in imitation of Racine, the encouragement of Victor Hugo, the romantic starvation in a garret. Not the mistress, however, for Verne was a fairly devout Catholic. It was not till he was in his thirties that Verne began to succeed, though later he was to make stupendous sums, particularly by the dramatised version of *Round the World in Eighty Days*. He did not die till 1905, his life almost exactly spanning the period between the first locomotive and the first aeroplane.

(*Facing page*) One of Leon Bennett's fine illustrations for *Robur le Conquérant*.

(*Below*) The Gun Club's invention to fire the rocket shell to the moon in *From the Earth to the Moon*.

Mr Allott's main theme is the relation between the cult of Science and the Romantic phase in literature. Although later he was to have misgivings — he was not altogether easy about the theory of evolution, for instance — Verne belongs to the early scientific period, the period of the Great Eastern and the Hyde Park Exhibition of 1851, when the key-phrase was 'Command over Nature' rather than, as now, 'Mysterious Universe'. The mechanical sciences were advancing at tremendous speed and their sinister possibilities were seldom foreseen. Until the invention of the Maxim gun it must have been difficult not to equate scientific invention with progress. One could hardly have a better illustration of the prevailing optimism of the time than the fact that the war of 1870 left Verne almost

unaffected. It appeared to him simply as a tiresome interruption, after which one could get on with one's work. The modern wars of extermination had not only started, but, no doubt, would have been difficult to imagine. Later, however Verne watched with disgust the rise of modern imperialism and the scramble for Africa. One result of this was the disappearance from his books of the sympathetic Englishman. In his earlier work this character appears over and over again — a queer figure, as in most nineteenth-century French novels, given to wearing check suits and breaking long silences with cries of 'Hip, hip, hurrah!' but symbolising the pragmatism and inventiveness which Verne admired in the English-speaking races.

It is difficult not to couple Verne's name with that of H. G. Wells, whom Mr Allott dislikes and goes out of his way to decry. Wells, even more than Verne, has made himself the apostle of Science, but he belongs to a less confident period in which the smallness of man against the background of the spiral nebulae is more obvious than his mastery over Nature. Well's early romances are less scientific than Verne's — that is, less close to the established knowledge of the time — but there is far more feeling of *wonder* in them. If one compares *A Journey to the Moon* with *The First Men in the Moon*, one sees the advantage, at any rate from a purely literary point of view, of a less anthropocentric standpoint. Verne's story is scientific, or very nearly so. Granted that one could fire a projectile out of the earth's gravitational pull, and that the human beings inside it could survive the shock, the thing might have happened as it is recorded. Wells's story is pure speculation, based on nothing except a predilection for thinking that the moon and the planets are inhabited. But it creates a universe of its own, which one remembers in detail years after reading it. The most memorable incident in Verne's book is the time when the oxygen cylinder sprang a leak and produced symptoms of drunkenness in the explorers — precisely the incident that tethers the story to the earth. In spite of Mr Allott's efforts, it seems doubtful whether Verne will be read much longer, except by schoolchildren 'doing' *A Journey to the Centre of the Earth* as

Fire! The rocket shell blasts off on its journey to the moon in *From the Earth to the Moon*. Also an illustration of the interior of the projectile.

The rocket shell traversing space in *From the Earth to the Moon* while its occupants experience the sensation of weightlessness. Safely back to earth — the first men to have gone from the earth to the moon land in the sea near a rescue vessel.

an alternative to *Tartarin of Tarascon*. He set out to combine instruction with entertainment, and he succeeded, but only so long as his scientific theories were more or less up to date. He does, however, enjoy a sort of anonymous immortality because of a controversy that has sprung out of one of his books. In *Round the World in Eighty Days* — itself based, as Mr Allott points out, on a short story of Poe's — he makes play with the fact that if one travels round the world eastward one gains a day in the passage. And this has given rise to the question, 'What will happen when an aeroplane can fly round the world in twenty-four hours?', which is much debated by imaginative boys, readers of the *Wizard* and the *Hotspur*, who have probably never heard Verne's name. This is an interesting book, in spite of its tendency to stray too far from its subject.

JULES VERNE AT HOME

by Marie Belloc

For much of his life, Verne lived as a virtual recluse in his tall, dark house in Amiens, allowing few visitors and imposing an almost total ban on journalists. He was almost disinterested in what was written about him, and when he was asked to write his autobiography because it was felt people would like to know more about him, he replied sharply, 'I do not agree . . . and I have never thought of doing it. An account of my travels would have very little interest for my readers, and the story of my life would have no more. A writer interests his public only as a writer.' In the autumn of 1894, Verne made something of an exception to his rule, although the interviewer in this instance was another writer — and a well-known one at that — Marie A. Belloc, the sister of Hilaire Belloc, and later to score a world-wide success with her novel *The Lodger* based on the Jack the Ripper murders. This charming and very attractive woman was allowed access to the author's home and later published the following intimate account of Verne's life, work and opinions in *The Strand Magazine*, February 1895.

The author of *Round the World in Eighty Days, Five Weeks in a Balloon,* and many other delightful stories which cannot but have endeared his personality to hundreds of thousands of readers in every part of the world, spends his happy, well-filled working life in Amiens, a quiet, French provincial town situated on the direct route from Calais and Boulogne to Paris.

The humblest Amienois can point out Jules Verne's home. No. 1, Rue Charles Dubois, is a charming, old-fashioned house, situated at the corner of a countrified street leading out of a broad boulevard.

The little door let into a lichen-covered wall was answered by a cheerful-looking old *bonne*. As soon as she heard that I had come by appointment, she led the way across a paved court-yard bounded on two sides by a picturesque, irregular building, flanked by the short tower which is so often a feature of French country houses. As a followed her, I was able to catch a glimpse of Jules Verne's garden, a distant vista of great beeches shading wide expanses of well-kept turf brilliant with flower-beds. Though it was late autumn; everything was exquisitely neat and dainty, and not a stray leaf was to be seen on the broad gravel paths, where the veteran novelist takes every day one of his frequent constitutionals.

A row of shallow stone steps leads to a conservatory hall, which, filled with palms and flowering shrubs, forms a pleasant ante-chamber to the beautiful *salon*, where I was joined a few moments later by my host and hostess.

As the famous author is the first to acknowledge, Mme Jules Verne has played no small part in each and all of her husband's triumphs and successes; and it is difficult to believe that the bright, active old lady, still so full of youthful vivacity and French *espieglerie*, can really have celebrated over a year ago her golden wedding.

Jules Verne, in his personal appearance, does not fulfil the popular idea of a great author. Rather does he give the impression of being a cultured country gentleman, and this notwithstanding the fact that he always dresses in the sombre black affected by most Frenchmen belonging to the professional classes. His coat is decorated with the tiny red button denoting that the wearer possesses the high distinction of being an officer of the Legion of Honour. As he sat talking he did not look his seventy-eight years, and, indeed, appeared but little changed since the large portrait, hanging opposite that of his wife, was painted some twenty odd years ago.

M. Verne is singularly modest about his work, and showed no desire to talk about either his books or himself. Had it not been for the kindly assistance of his wife, whose pride in her husband's genius is delightful to witness, I

Jules Verne's study – a photograph taken from the *Strand* magazine, as are those on the facing page of the author and his home in Amiens.

should have found it difficult to persuade him to give me any particulars about his literary career or his methods of work.

'I cannot remember the time,' he observed, in answer to a question, 'when I did not write, or intend to be an author; and as you will soon see, many things conspired to that end. You know, I am a Breton by birth – my native town being Nantes – but my father was a Parisian by education and taste, devoted to literature, and, although he was too modest to make any effort to popularize his work, a fine poet. Perhaps this is why I myself began my literary career by writing poetry, which – for I followed the example of most budding French litterateurs – took the form of a five-act tragedy,' he concluded, with a half-sigh – half-smile.

'My first real piece of work, however,' he added, after a pause, 'was a little comedy written in collaboration with Dumas *fils*, who was, and has remained, one of my best friends. Our play was called *Pailles Rompues* ('Split Straws'), and was acted at the Gymnase Theatre in Paris; but, although I much enjoyed light dramatic work, I did not find that it brought me anything in the way of substance or fortune.

'And yet,' he continued, slowly, 'I have never lost my love for the stage and everything connected with theatrical life. One of the keenest joys my story-writing has brought me has been the successful staging of some of my novels, notably *Michel Strogoff*.

'I have often been asked what first gave me the idea of writing what, for

the want of a better name, may be styled scientific romances.

'Well, I had always been devoted to the study of geography, much as some people delight in history and historical research. I really think that my love for maps and the great explorers of the world led to my composing the first of my long series of geographical stories.

An illustration from *The Second Fatherland* (1900) based on *Robinson Crusoe* whose adventures so delighted Verne as a child.

'When writing my first book, *Five Weeks in a Balloon*, I chose Africa as the scene of action, for the simple reason that less was, and is, known about that continent than any other; and it struck me that the most ingenious way in which this portion of the world's surface could be explored would be from a balloon. I thoroughly enjoyed writing the story, and, even more, I may add, the researches which it made necessary; for then, as now, I always tried to make even the wildest of my romances as realistic and true to life as possible.

'Once the story was finished, I sent the manuscript to the well-known Paris publisher, M. Hetzel. He read the tale, was interested by it, and made me an offer which I accepted. I may tell you that this excellent man and his son became, and have remained, my very good friends, and the firm are about to publish my fiftieth novel.'

'Then you passed no anxious moments waiting on fame?' I asked. 'Did your first book become immediately popular, both at home and abroad?'

'Yes,' he answered, modestly. *'Five Weeks in a Balloon* has remained to this day one of the most read of my stories, but you must remember that I was already a man of thirty-five when this book was published, and had been married for some eight years,' he concluded, turning to Mme Verne with a charming air of old-fashioned gallantry.

'Your love of geography did not prevent your possessing a strong bent for science?'

'Well, I do not in any way pose as a scientist, but I esteem myself fortunate

as having been born in an age of remarkable discoveries, and perhaps still more wonderful inventions.'

'You are doubtless aware,' interposed Mme Verne, proudly, 'that many apparently impossible scientific phenomena in my husband's romances have come true?'

'Tut, tut,' cried M. Verne, deprecatingly, 'that is a mere coincidence, and is doubtless owing to the fact that even when inventing scientific phenomena I always try and make everything seem as true and simple as possible. As to the accuracy of my descriptions, I owe that in a great measure to the fact that, even before I began writing stories, I always took numerous notes out of every book, newspaper, magazine, or scientific report that I came across. These notes were, and are, all classified according to the subject with which they dealt, and I need hardly point out to you how invaluable much of this material has been to me.

'I subscribe to over twenty newspapers,' he continued, 'and I am an assiduous reader of every scientific publication; even apart from my work I keenly enjoy reading or hearing about any new discovery or experiment in the worlds of science, astronomy, meteorology, or physiology.'

'And do you find that this miscellaneous reading suggests to you any new ideas for stories, or do you depend for your plots wholly on your own imagination?'

'It is impossible to say what suggests the skeleton of a story; sometimes one thing, sometimes another. I have often carried an idea in my brain for years before I had occasion to work it out on paper, but I always make a note when anything of the kind occurs to me. Of course, I can distinctly trace the beginnings of some of my books: *Round the World in Eighty Days* was the result of reading a tourist advertisement in a newspaper. The paragraph which caught my attention mentioned the fact that nowadays it would be quite possible for a man to travel round the world in eighty days, and it immediately flashed into my mind that the traveller, profiting by a difference of meridian, could be made to either gain or lose a day during that period of time. It was this initial thought that really made the whole point of the story. You will, perhaps, remember that my hero, Phileas Fogg, owing to this circumstance arrived home in time to win his wager, instead of, as he imagined, a day too late.'

'Talking of Phileas Fogg, monsieur: unlike most French writers, you seem to enjoy making your heroes of English or foreign extraction.'

'Yes, consider that members of the English-speaking race make excellent heroes, especially where a story of adventure, or scientific pioneering work, is about to be described. I thoroughly admire the pluck and go-ahead qualities of the nation which have planted the Union Jack on so great a portion of the earth's surface.'

'Your stories also differ from those of almost all your fellow-authors,' I ventured to observe, 'inasmuch that in them the fair sex plays so small a part.'

An approving glance from my kindly hostess showed me that she agreed with the truth of my observation.

'I deny that *in toto*,' cried M. Verne, with some heat. 'Look at *Mistress*

Charles Dickens was another influence on Verne, and this is particularly evident in the story *Foundling Mick* (1893).

Branican, and the charming young girls in some of my stories. Whenever there is any necessity for the feminine element to be introduced you will always find it there.' Then, smiling: 'Love is an all-absorbing passion, and leaves room for little else in the human breast; my heroes need all their wits about them, and the presence of a charming young lady might now and again sadly interfere with what they have to do. Again, I have always wished to so write my stories that they might be placed without the least hesitation in the hands of all young people, and I have scrupulously avoided any scene which, say, a boy would not like to think his sister would read.'

'Before daylight wanes, would you not like to come upstairs and see my husband's workroom and study?' asked my hostess; 'there we can continue our conversation.'

And so, with Mme Verne leading the way, we went once more through the light, airy hall, where a door opened straight on to the quaint winding staircase, which leads up and up till are reached the cosy set of rooms where M. Verne passes the greater part of his life, and from where have issued many of his most enchanting books. As we went along the passage, I noticed some large maps — dumb testimonies of their owner's delight in geography and love of accurate information — hanging on the wall.

'It is here,' remarked Mme Verne, throwing open the door of what proved to be a tiny, cell-like bedchamber, 'that my husband does his actual writing each morning. You must know that he gets up at five, and by lunch-time, that is, eleven o'clock, his actual writing, proof-correcting, and so on, are over for the day; but one cannot burn the candle at both ends, and each evening he is generally sound asleep by eight or half-past eight o'clock.'

The plain wooden desk-table is situated in front of the one large window, and opposite the little camp bed; between the pauses of his work on winter mornings M. Verne, by glancing up, is able to see the dawn breaking over the beautiful spire of Amiens Cathedral. The tiny room is bare of all ornamentation, save for two busts of Molière and Shakespeare, and a few pictures, including a watercolour of my host's yacht, the *St. Michel*, a splendid little boat in which he and his wife spent, some years ago, many of the happiest hours of their long dual life.

Opening out of the bedroom is a fine large apartment, Jules Verne's library. The room is lined with book-cases, and in the middle a large table groans under a carefully sorted mass of newspapers, reviews, and scientific reports, to say nothing of a representative collection of French and English periodical literature. A number of cardboard pigeon-holes, occupying however wonderfully little space, contain the twenty odd thousand notes garnered by the author during his long life.

'Tell me what are a man's books, and I will tell you what manner of man he is,' makes an excellent paraphrase of a good old saying, and might well be applied to Jules Verne. His library is strictly for use, not show, and well-worn copies of such intellectual friends as Homer, Virgil, Montaigne, and

Shakespeare, shabby, but how dear to their owner; editions of Fenimore Cooper, Dickens, and Scott show hard and constant usage; and there also, in newer dress, many of the better-known English novels have found their way.

'These books will show you,' observed M. Verne, genially, 'how sincere is my affection for Great Britain. All my life I have delighted in the works of Sir Walter Scott, and during a never-to-be-forgotten tour in the British Isles, my happiest days were spent in Scotland. I still see, as in a vision, beautiful, picturesque Edinburgh, with its Heart of Midlothian, and many entrancing memories; the Highlands, world-forgotten Iona, and the wild Hebrides. Of course, to one familiar with the works of Scott, there is scarce a district of his native land lacking some association connected with the writer and his immortal work.'

'And how did London impress you?'

'Well, I consider myself a regular devotee of the Thames. I think the great river is the most striking feature of that extraordinary city.'

'I should like to ask you your opinion of some of our boys' books and stories of adventure. Of course, you know England has led the van in regard to such literature.'

'Yes, indeed, notably with that classic, beloved alike by old and young, *Robinson Crusoe*; and yet perhaps I shall shock you by admitting that I myself prefer the dear old *Swiss Family Robinson*. People forget that Crusoe and his man Friday were but an episode in a seven-volumed story. To my mind the book's great merit is that it was apparently the first romance of the kind ever perpetrated. We have all written *Robinsons*,' he added, laughing; 'but it is a moot question if any of them would have seen the light had it not been for their famous prototype.'

'And where do you place other English writers of adventure?'

'Unhappily, I can read only those works which have been translated into French. I never tire of Fenimore Cooper; certain of his romances deserve true immortality, and will I trust be remembered long after the so-called literary giants of a later age are forgotten. Then, again, I thoroughly enjoy Captain Marryat's breezy romances. Owing to my unfortunate inability to read English, I am not so familiar as I should like to be with Mayne Read and Robert Louis Stevenson; still, I was greatly delighted with the latter's *Treasure Island*, of which I possess a translation. It seemed to me, when I read it, to possess extraordinary freshness of

The natives storming the castaways stronghold in *The Second Fatherland* – an example of Verne's love for *The Swiss Family Robinson*.
Charles Dickens, 'the master of storytellers' according to Verne.

style and enormous power. I have not mentioned,' he continued, 'the English writer whom I consider the master of them all, namely, Charles Dickens,' and the face of the King of Storytellers lit up with youthful enthusiasm. 'I consider that the author of *Nicholas Nickleby, David Copperfield*, and *The Cricket on the Hearth* possesses pathos, humour, incident, plot, and descriptive power, any one of which might have made the reputation of a less gifted mortal; but here, again, is one of those whose fame may smoulder but will never die.'

Whilst her husband was concluding these remarks, Mme Verne drew my attention to a large book-case filled with rows of apparently freshly bound and little-read books. 'Here,' she observed, 'are various French, German, Portuguese, Dutch, Swedish, and Russian editions of M. Verne's books, including a Japanese and Arab translation of *Round the World in Eighty Days*, and my kindly hostess took down and opened the strange vellum-bound pages wherein each little Arab who runs may read of the adventures of Phileas Fogg, Esq.

'My husband,' she added, 'has never re-read a chapter of a single one of his stories. When the last proofs are corrected his interest in them ceases, and this, although he has sometimes been thinking over a plot, and inventing situations figuring in a story, during years of his life.'

'And what, monsieur, are your methods of work?' I inquired. 'I suppose you can have no objection to giving away your recipe?'

'I cannot see,' he answered, good-humouredly, 'what interest the public can find in such things; but I will initiate you into the secrets of my literary kitchen, though I do not know that I would recommend anybody else to proceed on the same plan; for I always think that each of us works in his or her own way, and instinctively knows what method is best. Well, I start by making a draft of what is going to be my new story. I never begin a book without knowing what the beginning, the middle, and the end will be. Hitherto I have always been fortunate enough to have not one, but half-a-dozen definite schemes floating in my mind. If I ever find myself hard up for a subject, I shall consider that it is time for me to give up work. After having completed my preliminary draft, I draw up a plan of the chapters, and then begin the actual writing of the first rough copy in pencil, leaving a half-page margin for corrections and emendations; I then read the whole, and go over all I have already done in ink. I consider that my real labour begins with my first set of proofs, for I not only correct something in every sentence, but I rewrite whole chapters. I do not seem to have a grip of my subject till I see my work in print; fortunately, my kind publisher allows me every latitude as regards corrections, and I often have as many as eight or nine revises. I envy, but do not attempt to emulate the example of those who from the time they write Chapter 1 to the word Finis, never see reason to alter or add a single word.'

'This method of composition must

A dramatic moment from *The Mutineers* a short story which was Verne's first published effort at prose fiction.

greatly retard your work?'

'I do not find it so. Thanks to my habits of regularity, I invariably produce two completed novels a year. I am also always in advance of my work; in fact, I am now writing a story which properly belongs to my working year 1897; in other words, I have five manuscripts ready for the printers. Of course,' he added, thoughtfully, 'this has not been achieved without sacrifice. I soon found real hard work and a constant, steady rate of production incompatible with the pleasures of society. When we were younger, my wife and myself lived in Paris, and

Jules Verne delighted in spending time afloat and this is reflected in novels like *The Pilot of the Danube* (1908).

enjoyed the world and its manifold interests to the full. During the last twelve years I have become a towns-man of Amiens; my wife is an Amienoise by birth. It was here that I first made her acquaintance, fifty-three years ago, and little by little all my affections and interests have centred in the town. Some of my friends will even tell you that I am far prouder of being a town councillor of Amiens than of my literary reputation. I do not deny that I thoroughly enjoy taking my share in municipal government.'

'Then, have you never followed the example of so many of your own personages, and travelled, as you easily might have done, here, there, and everywhere?'

'Yes, indeed; I am passionately fond of travelling, and at one time spent a considerable portion of each year on my yacht, the *St. Michel*. Indeed, I may say I am devoted to the sea, and I can imagine nothing more ideal than a sailor's life; but with age came a strong love of peace and quietude, and,' added the veteran novelist, half sadly, 'I now journey only in imagination.'

'I believe, monsieur, that you add the dramatist's laurels to your other triumphs?'

'Yes,' he answered; 'you know we have in France a proverb which declares that a man always ends by returning to his old love. Well, as I told you before, I always took a special delight in everything dramatic, and made my literary début as a play-wright, and of the many substantial

A MUSE TO SCOTLAND

Although Jules Verne set his stories in virtually every country of the world, he actually travelled very little himself, relying to a great extent on research into any localities he chose. However, one of the few trips he did make was in 1859 when he was invited to visit Britain. The highlight of this trip was the time he spent in Scotland — particularly as he had been since his childhood an admirer of Sir Walter Scott — and he found inspiration in both the beautiful scenery as well as the depressed social conditions. From the desolate coal mines came the novel, *Child of the Cavern* (1877), and from the picturesque Hebrides, *The Green Ray* (1883). Indeed, so impressed was he by the country, that he was even moved to write a short poem which is reprinted below.

Lovely lakes with sleeping waters
   Keep forever
Your charming legends,
   Lovely Scottish lakes!
On your shores we find the tracks
Of those heroes so greatly regretted,
Those descendants of a noble race
Of whom our Walter has sung!
Here is the tower of the witches
Preparing their frugal meal;
There, the vast fields of heather
To which the shade of Fingal returns.

Here occur in the sombre night
The mad dances of the fairies;

There, sinister, appears in the gloom
The face of the old Puritans!
And amidst the wild rocks,
In the evening you may still surprise
Waverley, who towards your shores
Attracts Flora MacIvor!

The Lady of the Lakes is doubtless
   coming.
Roaming on her palfrey,
And Diana, not far away, can listen to
The sounds of Rob Roy's horn!
Have we not even yet heard
Fergus in the midst of his clans,
Sounding the pibroch of war,

Once more awakening the echo from
   the Highlands?
So far from you, poetic lakes,
Fate is turning our steps.
Ravines, boulders, ancient caves,
Our eyes will never forget you!
Oh vision too quickly ended
Cannot return to us!
Farewell, ancient Caledonia,
Farewell, all our memories!

Lovely lakes with sleeping waters
   Keep forever
Your charming legends,
   Lovely Scottish lakes!   *Jules Verne*

---

satisfactions brought me by my labours, none gave more pleasure than my return to the stage.'

'And which of your stories were most successful in dramatic form?'

'*Michel Strogoff* was perhaps the most popular; it was played all over the world; then *Round the World in Eighty Days* was very successful, and more lately *Mathias Sandorf* was acted in Paris; it may amuse you to know further that my *Doctor Ox* formed the basis of an operetta at the Variétés some seventeen years ago. I was once able to superintend the mounting of my pieces myself; now, my only glimpse of the theatrical world is seen from the front, in our charming Amiens theatre, on the, I must admit, frequent occasions when some good provincial company honours our town with its presence.'

'I suppose,' I observed to Mme Verne, 'that your husband receives many communications from his immense English constituency of unknown friends and readers?'

'Yes, indeed,' she cried, brightly; 'and the applications for autographs! I wish you could see them. If I were not there to save him from his friends, he would spend most of his time writing out his name on slips of paper. I suppose few people have received stranger epistles than my husband. People write to him about all sorts of things: they suggest plots for new stories, they confide to him their troubles, they tell him their adventures, and they send him their books.'

'And do those unknown correspondents ever permit themselves to ask indiscreet questions about M. Verne's future plans?'

My good-natured and courteous host answered for her, 'Many are so kind as to be interested in my next book; if you share that curiosity, you may care to know what I have not yet announced to any but my intimates, namely, that my next story will have for title, *L'Ile Hélice* — in English, *Screw Island*. It embodies a set of notions and ideas that have been in my mind for many years. The action will take place on a floating island created by the ingenuity of man, a kind of *Great Eastern* magnified 10,000 times, and containing, of course, the whole of what in this case may be truly called a moving population. It is my intention,' concluded M. Verne, 'to complete, before my working days are done, a series which shall conclude in story form my whole survey of the world's surface and the heavens; there are still left corners of the world to which my thoughts have not yet penetrated. As you know, I have dealt with the moon, but a great deal remains to be done, and if health and strength permit me, I hope to finish the task.'

THE BIZARRE GENIUS OF EDGAR POE

by Jules Verne

Several writers influenced Jules Verne – including Scott, Fenimore Cooper and Dickens – but certainly none more so than that strange American genius, Edgar Allan Poe. In 1864 Verne paid tribute to the man in a special article for the magazine *Musée de Familles*, to which he contributed a number of essays both under his own name and anonymously. One of Verne's biographers, Marguerite Allotte de la Fuye, believes this item is 'particularly revealing' and says ot it in her book, 'It is only like natures that influences us, and the genius of Poe certainly corresponded to some of Jules Verne's deepest leanings: his curiosity about numbers; his knowledge of ciphers and codes; tne attraction which the problems of the unknowable exerted upon him; his taste for fantastic, hallucinatory and mystifying adventures; his soaring flight into the infinite of future possibilities; to which he added the urge to discover a lucid explanation for the most obscure enigmas. Jules Verne thus paid homage both to the American writer and to his translator, Baudelaire, whom he hailed as leaders in the school of the strange and supernatural.' As this essay is both very long and contains numerous extracts from the original Poe stories which are scarcely relevant here, this specially edited translation has been prepared by the well-known Verne authority, I. O. Evans. Poe's influence on Verne can, of course, be seen most strongly in stories such as *Five Weeks in a Balloon* (based on *The Balloon Hoax*), *Mathias Sandorf* (which dwells on hypnotism like *The Facts in the Case of M. Valdemar*), *From Earth to the Moon* (*The Adventure of one Hans Pfaall*) and *Round the World in Eighty Days* (using the same concept as *Three Sundays in a Week*). Verne also completed Poe's unfinished novel, *Arthur Gordon Pym* in *The Sphinx of the Icefields*.

A superb illustration by A. D. McCormick for an 1898 American edition of Edgar Allan Poe's *Arthur Gordon Pym*.

Here, my dear readers, is an American novelist with a great reputation. Many of you, no doubt, will be familiar with his name, but few will know his work. Permit me, then, to tell you something about the man and his work; both occupy a high position in the history of the imagination, for Edgar Poe has created a distinct species of this, originating with himself, and of which he seems to have borne away the secret. You might call him, 'The Leader of the Cult of the Unusual'; he has thrust back the bounds of what is impossible. He will certainly have imitators; those who seek to go beyond him, to exaggerate his style; but plenty of those who fancy that they have surpassed him, will not even have equalled him.

People have sometimes compared him with two other authors; one is English, Anne Radcliffe, the other German, Hoffman. But Mrs Radcliffe has exploited the *type terrible* which explains everything by natural causes;

Hoffman has indulged in fantasy, for which no natural cause can be adduced. This is not the style of Poe; his characters seem really to exist; they are pre-eminently human, though sometimes they show that they were endowed with an over-excitable sensibility — super-nervous, exceptionally individualistic, one might say galvanised, as people are who have breathed air too rich in oxygen, and whose life seems always to be actually on fire. If they are not insane, the characters of Poe seem likely to become insane through having abused their brain just as others have abused alcoholic liquors; they push to the limit the urge to ponder and deduce; they are the most formidable analysts that I know of, and when seized by a brilliant idea they reach an irrefutable truth.

As I said, Poe has drawn varied effects with his bizarre imagination and I am going to sketch the main ones quickly by quoting a few stories. Stories such as *Ms Found in a Bottle*, the fantastic description of a shipwreck in which every wreck is collected by an impossible vessel manned by shades; *A Descent into the Maelstrom*, a dizzy exploit attempted by the Lofoden fisherman; *The Facts in the Case of M Valdemar*, the story of the death of a man deferred by a mesmeric sleep; *The Black Cat*, the tale of an assassin whose crime is revealed by that animal clumsily buried with the victim; *The Man of the Crowd*, an exceptional person who lives only in crowds, and whom Poe, attracted in spite of himself, follows in London from the morning onwards, through the rain and fog, through crowded streets, in noisy bazaars, in groups of rioters, in secluded places where the drunkards collect, everywhere where there is a crowd, his natural element; and *The Fall of the House of Usher* a terrifying experience of a young girl who is believed to be dead, who is buried, and then recovers.

Then there are the three stories in which his skill in analysing and deducing reached the utmost bounds of intelligence, *The Murders in the Rue Morgue*, *The Purloined Letter* and *The Gold Bug*. The last named is a particularly strange and astounding story, arousing interest by methods hitherto

George Roux provided this picture for Verne's continuation of the Poe story, *The Sphinx of the Icefields* (1897).

A Portrait of Edgar Allan Poe, the man Verne so admired, by Frederick Halpin.

unknown and by strictly logical deductions, and which, in itself, is enough to illustrate the American novelist. To my mind it is the most remarkable of all his strange stories; for in this is revealed the supreme degree of that kind of literature which has become 'the Poe Type'.

I must now mention *The Balloon Hoax* which I will tell you in a few lines is about a flight across the Atlantic. The report of this voyage appeared in the *New Yok Sun*. Many people believed in it who certainly had not read it, for the method Poe described, the Archimedean screw, which acted as a propeller, and the rudder, would have been absolutely insufficient to steer a balloon. The aeronauts, who had set out from England

As you know, it is the pressure of the air which lifts the aerostat. Reaching the upper limits of the atmosphere, six thousand fathoms or thereabouts, a balloon, if it could reach it, would stop short, and no human force would make it go higher. It was there that Pfaall, or rather Poe himself, enters into long arguments to show that outside the layers of air there extends another medium, the ether. These discussions are made with a remarkable assurance, and the arguments are based on what are almost fallacies, with the most illogical force. Briefly, he arrives at the conclusion that there is a strong probability that at no period of its flight would the various weights of that immense balloon and its accessories, of the inconceivably rare gas that it contains, its car and contents, be exactly equal to the surrounding atmosphere which it displaces.

Here is the basic assumption; but that is not sufficient. Indeed to rise, always to rise, that is all very well; but it is also necessary to breathe; so Pfaall takes along a certain contrivance made to condense the atmosphere, however rare it may be, sufficiently for the needs of respiration. Very well, here is an air which it is necessary to condense to supply the lungs, and which, however, will be dense enough in its natural state to raise the balloon. You will understand how these facts contradict one another.

Nevertheless, once the basic assumptions are admitted, the journey of Pfaall is wonderfully described, packed with unexpected comments and strange observations. Poe, of course, ended his tale by showing it was nothing but a hoax!

I must also cite the story entitled *Three Sundays in a Week*. It is of a type not so sad but bizarre. How can there be a week with three Sundays? Easily for three individuals, and Poe demonstrates this. Briefly, the Earth is twenty-five thousand miles in circumference, and it turns on its axis from east to west in twenty-four hours; this is a speed of about a thousand miles an hour. Let us assume that the first person sets out from London, and goes a thousand miles towards the west; he sees the sun an hour before the person who stays where he is. At the end of a thousand more miles, he sees it two hours earlier; at the end of his tour around the world, returned to his point of departure, he will be just a whole day in advance of the second person. And if the third person carries out the same voyage in the same conditions, but in the opposite direction, by going towards the east, after his tour around the world he will be a day later.

for Paris, were swept into America as far as Sullivan's Island and during their voyage they attained a height of 25,000 feet. The story was short, and the incidents of the voyage were reproduced in an account more strange than it is true.

I prefer *The Unparalleled Adventures of one Hans Pfaall* although I must hasten to tell you that, here again, the most elementary laws of physics and mechanics are boldly transgressed. This has always seemed astonishing to me as coming from Poe, who, by a few inventions, could have made his story more plausible. After all, as it deals with a voyage to the moon, the mode of transport need not have been too

Two sketches by the French film-maker Georges Méliès of his 'Giant of the Snows' which featured in his movie, *The Conquest of the Pole* (1912) and was based on Verne's *The Sphinx of the Icefields.*

difficult. I must tell you how Pfaall accomplished that impossible flight. To meet his needs, he had filled his balloon with a gas invented by himself, produced by the combination of a certain metallic substance, or demi-metal, and of a very common acid. This gas was one of the constituents of azote, hitherto considered irreducible, and its density was thirty-seven times that of hydrogen. Here we are, then, speaking physically, in the realm of phantasy; but that's not everything.

So what happens if the three of them meet on Sunday at their starting-point? For the first, *yesterday* was Sunday; for the second, *today*; and for the third, it is *tomorrow*. As you see, this is a cosmographic joke explained in remarkable words.

Finally, I reach the story with which I shall end this study of Poe's works. It is longer than the other stories and bears the title, *Adventures of Arthur Gordon Pym*. Perhaps more human than the Strange Stories, it is no less unusual for all that. It shows situations which are not to be found anywhere else, and its character is essentially dramatic. It is a tale of a strange sea voyage which ends mysteriously in mid-sentence in the wild, snow-world of the Antarctic.

Who will ever complete it? Someone bolder than myself, and more rash to advance into the domain of impossibilities. Yet we must believe that Gordon Pym managed to get away because he himself wrote this strange publication; but he died before having completed his work. Poe appears to regret this very sorely and declines the task of filling up the gap. [In spite of this emphatic statement, Verne himself completed Poe's narrative in 1895 under the title, *Le Sphinx des Glaces*. He also dedicated the work to the memory of Poe and *'mes amis d'Amerique.'* Editor's note.]

These, then, are the chief works of the American novelist; have I gone too far in calling them strange and supernatural? Has he not created a new form of literature, a form which demonstrates the delicacy of excessive mind, to use one of his own words?

Leaving the incomprehensibilities on one side, that which we have to

Another fabulous sea beast featured in *Les Histoires de Jean-Marie Cabidoulin* which has not surprisingly become better known under the title of *The Sea Serpent* (1901).

admire in the works of Poe are the originality of his situations, his discussion of little-known facts, his observation of the morbid faculties of man, his choice of subjects, the ever-strange personalities of his heroes, their nervous temperament, their way of expressing themselves by bizarre interjections. And yet in the midst of these impossibilities, there still sometimes exists an appearance of reality which takes possession of the reader's belief.

May I also be allowed to call attention to the materialistic aspect of his stories; they never suggest providential intervention. Poe never seems to admit to this; he claims to explain everything by physical laws, which he will even

invent if he has to; we never feel in him that faith which could have been given him by ceaseless contemplation of the supernatural. He creates his fantasies *coldly*, if I may express myself in this way, and the poor man is always an apostle of materialism. But I imagine this is less the fault of his temperament than the influence of the exclusively practical and industrial society of the United States. He wrote, thought and dreamed as an American, this positivist of a man. But this tendency being admitted, let us wholeheartedly admire his work.

(*Below and left*) A frame from the film *Five Weeks In A Balloon* (1962) and a photograph taken on the set of the out-of-shot crane which actually enabled the exotic flying machine to take off! (*Above*) An illustration from a recent juvenile edition of *Five Weeks In A Balloon*. Ballooning also featured in a dramatic short story which Verne wrote entitled *A Drama In The Air*.

THE 'INSOLUBLE' CIPHER

It was from Edgar Allan Poe that Verne gained his interest in ciphers, and he introduced them into three particular novels, *Journey to the Centre of the Earth* (1864), *Mathias Sandorf* (1885) and most importantly, *The Giant Raft* which is about a floating island in South America (1881). In the Second Part of this novel, 'The Cryptogram', the story revolves around the solving of a cipher to save an innocent man from hanging. Verne was apparently very proud of this code which he believed completely insolveable and when his publisher, Hetzel, complained that he could not understand it, replied, 'In *The Gold Bug* which is only thirty pages long, ten pages are given up to figures, and Edgar Poe knew very well that the code was the whole point of the story, and yet a man's life didn't depend on it.' During the publication of the serial version of the story, Verne was amazed to learn that a student at *l'Ecole Polytechnique* had actually managed to decipher the cryptogram before the appearance of the final chapters. 'What analytical power! I'm literally confounded,' he announced publicly, but complained privately to Hetzel that there must have been a leak at the printers. In any event the student's method was apparently lost — it was certainly never published — and Verne himself left no notes as to how he had devised the code. In subsequent editions of the book in French and English, there have been several suggestions offered as to how the deciphering *might* have been carried out, but only recently has a really practical solution been offered by a Verne enthusiast, H. J. Hardy, who presented it to I. O. Evans after his translation of *The Giant Raft* appeared in 1968. This marks the first publication of Mr Hardy's method and it provides what I consider a final solution for the biggest puzzle Verne created in his fiction and an answer to a real mystery he left at his death.

These two illustrations are from the first French edition of *The Giant Raft* (1881).

'*Phyjslyddqfdzxgasgzzqqehx gkfndrxujugiocytdxvksbxhhuy pohdvyrymhuhpuydkjoxphetoz sletnpmvffovpdpajxhyynojygg aymeqynfuqlnmvlyfgsuzmqiztl bqgyugsqeubvnrcredgruzblrmx yuhqhpzdrrgcrohepqxufivvrplp honthvddqfhqsntzhhhnfepmqk yuuexktogzgkyuumfvijdqdpzjq sykrplxhxqrymvklohhhotozvdk sppsuvjhd.*'

In this cipher, the frequency of count of all letters utterly rules out all possible hope of this being a simple substitution cypher. It will also be fairly clear that some form of substitution must be involved, since any form of plain transposition is also ruled out by the letters that appear.

There are several other basic types

of cipher that are possible and likely: not all involve a key used in the manner of this example. But a standard procedure in all, or at any rate most of them, is to look and see what digrams, trigrams, tetagrams, and longer sequences appear in the cipher. This I have done, it may not be 100% accurate but it is substantially correct, and good enough for the purpose:

1st letter	Frequency of following letter:	TOTAL
A	H–1 V–1 Q–1 //	3
C	H–2 R–2 S–2 Y–1 //	7
B	B–1 C–1 I–1 V–1 W–1 //	5
D	W–2 D–1 F–1 H–1 N–1 P1 Q–1 R–1 —1 (Last letter) //	10
E	M–1 Q–1 R–1 V–1 //	4
F	D–2 F–2 O–2 Q–2 S–2 V–2 J–1 N–1 T–1 //	15
G	W–4 C–2 G–2 X–2 B–1 R–1 S–1 V–1 //	14
H	H–3 L–3 P–3 W–2 Y–2 A–1 D–1 F–1 I–1 M–1 S–1 U–1 V–1 X–1 //	22
I	H–2 F–1 J–1 L–1 M–1 Q–1 R–1 U–1 V–1 X–1 //	11
J	J–4 R–3 H–2 N–2 V–2 F–1 O–1 W–1 Z–1 //	17
K	G–3 K–2 X–2 Q–1 S–1 V–1 //	10
L	C–2 G–1 I–1 K–1 R–1 X–1 Z–1 //	8

1st letter	Frequency of following letter:	TOTAL
M	F–3 W–2 G–1 E–1 U–1 //	8
N	T–2 D–1 H–1 X–1 //	5
O	H–3 G–2 L–1 P–1 W–1 //	8
P	D–2 Q–2 F–1 L–1 K–1 O–1 V–1 Y–1 //	10
Q	G–2 H–2 W–2 X–2 I–1 J–1 P–1 S–1 //	12
R	R–5 H–2 J–2 P–2 V–2 W–2 A–1 G–1 O–1 Z–1 //	19
S	E–2 U–2 B–1 H–1 I–1 J–1 K–1 Q–1 //	11
T	Z–2 G–1 H–1 L–1 O–1 //	6
U	B–1 C–1 H–1 L–1 M–1 Q–1 U–1 V–1 X–1 //	9
V	M–3 I–2 R–2 B–1 D–1 G–1 H–1 J–1 O–1 T–1 X–1 Y–1 //	16
W	J–4 F–3 S–2 Y–2 A–1 L–1 N–1 P–1 Q–1 T–1 U–1 W–1 //	19
X	K–3 F–2 D–1 J–1 P–1 T–1 U–1 V–1 W–1 Z–1 //	13
Y	I–3 F–1 J–1 U–1 Z–1 //	7
Z	R–2 B–1 G–1 M–1 O–1 V–1 //	7

Further examination of the digrams that occur twice or more reveals that the following trigrams are found more than once XKG (3 times), and WJJ and VMF (twice each). It also reveals that the sequence of twelve letters, RHYIHHLCRPQG occurs twice.

It is almost certain that this twelve letter sequence represents the same plaintext in both cases; the odds against it appearing just by a coincidence of two passages enciphered in two different ways to produce the same result are enormous. The same is true to a lesser extent of the trigrams, and even a number of digrams are likely to represent identical digrams in the plaintext, though here there will certainly be some that have just happened at random.

The next test will reveal whether the cryptogram is indeed constructed on the principle of a fixed number of definite separate methods of encipherment used in sequence, returning to the first when the series is exhausted. It is this. First, number consecutively every letter in the cryptogram. Then, take the numbers of the first letters of any sequences that are repeated and there-fore likely to represent the same plaintext. Subtract the smaller from the greater and if there is a key or any fixed number of different methods or encipherment used in sequence, then the number of different ciphers or the length of the key will be a factor (arithmetically) of the difference resulting from the said subtraction. This is because the series in the meanwhile has inevitably been used a complete number of times, as the same bit of sequence has twice enciphered the same fragment of original, to produce the same result in the cryptogram. If the difference is prime, then certainly a different method is in use. If not, one must examine other sequences, and these will reveal whether or not there is any common factor, bearing in mind that just one or two irreconcilable sequences might merely indicate that they have happened at random anyway and are not important any longer.

Applying this to the present cryptogram, the following is made known: in respect of the sequence RHYIHHLCR-POQH, it begins on numbers 14 and 218, giving a difference of 204, the factors of which being $17 \times 3 \times 2 \times 2$.

A gruesome clue in the search for buried treasure which ranges across Europe, the Middle East and West Africa in *Captain Antifer* (1894).

This gives possible key-lengths of 2, 3, 4, 6, 12, 17, 34, 51 etc. Of these key-lengths above 17 are most unlikely, but it is safer to examine the trigrams before coming to a definite conclusion. The XKG trigram begins on numbers 1, 49 and 181, yielding differences of 48 and 132, which factorize into $3 \times 2 \times 2 \times 2 \times 2$ and $11 \times 3 \times 2 \times 2$ respectively. A fixed key-length is now revealed as a decided possibility, with possible lengths of 2, 3, 4, 6 and 12. The trigram WJJ begins on letters 38 and 80: a difference of $42 -$, the factors being $7 \times 3 \times 2$, which tells against a length of 4 or 12 and in favour of a length of 2, 3 or 6.

This is confirmed by examination of the VMF trigram which begins on numbers 69 and 201. The difference here is 132, and that also is divisible by 2, 3 or 6. A fixed length of 6 is by far the most likely chance. Lengths of 2 and 3 though possible are inordinately short, and in addition they would be far more likely to reveal a greater number of repeated trigrams than appears in this cryptogram. What is more, if the key were in fact 2 or 3, one would expect to find at least one difference divisible by 2 or 3 alone. I have therefore arranged the cryptogram into 6 columns. It is then discovered that a considerable number of the digrams also fit the 6 length as will be apparent from the fact that many duplications occur in the same two columns:

JULES VERNE

The unravelling of clues also play a part in these three Verne novels.
(*Above*) *Un Billet du Loterie*, 1886; (*below*) *The Journey to the Centre of the Earth* (1864) and (*bottom*) the American Civil War story, *North Against South* (1887).

JOURNEY TO THE CENTRE OF THE EARTH

1	X	K	G	W	F	D	p
7	P	D	W	Y	I	R	v
13	V	R	H	Y	I	H	h
19	H	L	C	R	P	Q	h
25	H	U	Q	G	C	H	v
31	V	B	C	S	E	R	j
37	J	W2	J	J	N	X	v
43	V	G	G	W	P	I	x
49	X	K	G	X	P	O	h
55	H	L	G	W	T	H	w
61	W	F	Q	W	Y	L	r
67	R	J	V	M	F	F	s
73	S	Q	X	T	Z	R	r
79	R	W	J	J	O	L	k
85	K	K	V	G	T	W	a
91	A	H	P	Y	Z	V	i
97	I	F	Q	S	E	M	e
103	E	Q	W	F	S	B	i
109	I	L	I	M	U	H	i
115	I	Q	J	Z	O	G	v
121	V	H	F	F	O	O	v
127	X	Z	G	S	U	B	w
133	W	L	Z	B	B	V	r
139	R	R	V	O	P	D	q
145	Q	G	C	H	P	V	x
151	X	D	W	S	K	K	E
157	W	W	N	D	D	R	r
163	R	G	G	R	O	H	h
169	H	W	Q	I	J	H	m
175	M	W	Y	F	T	L	x
181	X	K	G	B	S	H	x
187	X	F	J	J	E	V	i
193	I	U	X	F	O	W	s
199	S	I	V	M	F	D	h
205	H	P	K	S	J	V	y
211	Y	U	C	Y	J	R	r
217	R	R	H	Y	I	H	h
223	H	L	C	R	P	Q	h
229	H	G	K	X	U	U	m
235	M	F	V	D	F	O	m
241	M	D	N	T	O	H	a
247	A	K	Q	X	J	J	r
253	R	W	J	N	T	Z	m
259	M	W	J	R	Z	R	a
265	A	Q	P	F	N	H	s
271	S	U	V	J	H	D	—

12 letter sequence
RHYIHHLCRPQH

The seventh column in lower case type is simply the first column repeated so as to see at a glance digrams that repeat on columns 6 and 1. It will be seen that in some digrams and trigrams there is at least one repetition in the same columns. For instance the WJJ trigram occurs twice, each time in columns 2, 3 and 4. (lines 37 and 79). Further, the WJ digram occurs twice more in columns 2 and 3 (lines 253 and 259). Incidentally, such a digram of this frequency is excellent material for TH, the most common digram in English.

12 letter sequence
RHYIHHLCRPQH

This method so far will apply to any cipher constructed on the principle of a fixed number of different encipherments used in sequence: whether on a shifted alphabet or a system more complicated. Whatever the system, it will be apparent that any given letter in the cryptogram will represent the same letter in the plaintext if the two or more identical letters are in the same column. If 'H' represents 'D' at one point in column 1, it will do so throughout it.

Looking at column 1, we find that X occurs 6 times, of which 3 are at the head of a trigram XKG. This trigram is excellent material for THE, the most common trigram of all, especially as it opens the paragraph. The words 'the', 'these', 'they', 'there', 'therefore', 'then', etc. are words that could well begin a paragraph. Tentatively adopting T for X in column 1, the next step is to make a frequency count for that column alone. The result of this is as follows:

A	B	C	D	E	F	G	H	I		J	K	L	M	N	O	P	Q	R		S	T	U	V	W	X	Y	Z
3	0	0	0	1	0	0	7	4		1	1	0	4	0	0	0	1	6		3	0	0	4	3	6	1	0

If the column is enciphered on a sliding alphabet, all plaintext letters will be 4 earlier than those in the cryptogram, adopting T for X, which is 4 letters back in the alphabet. This is easily checked by seeing what plaintext frequencies would result, and whether they are compatible with normal frequencies in English. The frequent letters here are A, H, I, M, R, S, V, W and X. If we apply a shifted alphabet of 4, we find them equivalent to W, D, E, I, N, O, R, S and T respectively. This is encouraging, for all these (except W) are very common indeed. Indeed the letters A, D, E, H, I, L, N, O, R, S and T normally make up over 70%

of all letters in use. Let us also look at the letters we would expect to find rarely, if at all. The least common letters in English are X, Z, B, J, K, P, Q and V. These would appear in the cryptogram as B, D, F, N, O, T, U and Z respectively, and it is very significant indeed that these are all highly conspicuous by their absence. It is safe to assume that a shifted alphabet of four has been used in column 1.

It is now fair to assume that a shifted alphabet has been used in all six columns, and all that is necessary to find out the various numbers by which the alphabet has been shifted. Turning to column 2, we find frequencies in the cryptogram as follows:

The clues that begin *The Journey to the Centre of the Earth* – an illustrated version of the story published by Pendulum Press, 1974.

A	B	C	D	E	F	G	H	I		J	K	L	M	N	O	P	Q	R		S	T	U	V	W	X	Y	Z
0	1	0	3	0	4	4	2	1		1	5	5	0	0	0	1	4	3		0	0	4	0	7	0	0	1

The frequent letters are D, F, G, H, K, L, Q, R, U and W. If one accepts the XKG trigram as representing THE as before, giving a shift of 3, the common letters in plaintext will be A, C, D, E, H,

I, N, O, R and T. Again these are all part of the very high frequency group (except C, which is borderline) so this test is encouraging. Further the rare letter group, X, Z, B, J, K, P, Q and V,

would appear in the cryptogram as A, C, E, M, N, S, T and Y, which do not appear in the column.

The rest of the cipher follows automatically. Trying E for G in column 3 will cause us to notice that the HLC which occurs twice in columns 1–3 is rendered DIA, followed by a D after 3 more letters. This leads one to suspect the word DIAMOND in both cases, especially in view of the story. Further, an alignment of RPQ as MON will also give THE for the repeated trigram YIH, and the sequences of 12 are therefore in both cases OF THE DIAMOND, and the key is 432513. A full test (which I should have done on a full group of 2 or 4 columns beforehand had there been any doubt) will reveal the full message as follows:

'The real author of the diamond robbery and the murder of the soldiers escorting the convoy on the night of twenty second January eighteen hundred and twenty six was not Joam da Costa, unjustly condemned to die. It was I, the wretched servant of the administration of the diamond district. Yes, I alone who sign this with my own name. "ORTEGA".'

The only minor error is a 'U' for the first 'T' in administration and minor errors of this type are inevitable in a cryptogram of this length. It is remarkable that that is the sole mistake; 5 or 6 would be usual.

(*Bottom*) James Mason, who has starred in several film versions of Verne stories, leading his party on *The Journey to the Centre of the Earth* (1954).
(*Facing page*) Four of the superb illustrations by A. De Neuville for Hetzel's first edition of *Vingt Mille Lieues sous les Mers* (1864).

Colourful illustrations for versions of
Twenty Thousand Leagues Under The Sea
published almost a century apart. The picture of the *Nautilus* slipping under the
waves is from an early English edition illustrated by Henry Austin, while the decor-
ative cover appeared on another edition a
quarter of a century later. The dramatic
cover for the picture strip version by Marvel
Comics was published in 1976

Naming Nemo

CAPTAIN NEMO, hero of Jules Verne's **20,000 Leagues Under the Sea**, was really a French revolutionary from the era of the Paris Commune in 1870. Indeed, his undersea adventures had to be carefully disguised to avoid running foul of French censorship after the Commune was smashed. This startling theory appears in the Moscow illustrated weekly **Ogonyok**, where historian Ilya Ginzburg links Nemo to Gustave Flourens—scientist, supporter of Greek revolts against the Turks in 1866, and a great friend of Mrs Karl Marx.

Newspaper cutting from *The Sunday Times,* March 5th 1978.

(*Top*) A rare still from *Under The Seas,* a lampoon of *Twenty Thousand Leagues Under The Sea* made by Georges Méliès in 1907.

(*Left*) An interesting still of the *Nautilus* as constructed for the version of the film made in 1937 by Universal.

(*Below*) James Mason as Captain Nemo starring in the 1954 Walt Disney film of the book – with a fascinating sketch of his submarine.

MY JOURNEY AROUND THE WORLD

by Thomas Cook

The book which made Jules Verne an international success as well as a wealthy man was *Around the World in Eighty Days* (1873) which is now widely regarded as the most famous of all his titles. The idea for the story had come to him during the summer of 1871 while he was working on the Paris Bourse. He had seen a promotional leaflet issued by the London travel agency of Thomas Cook which stated that transportation facilities now existed which made it possible for anyone to travel around the world. Cook himself was so convinced of the feasibility of his plan, the brochure stated, that he was now inviting applications for such a journey which he would personally conduct in the autumn of 1872. During the next year Verne devised the story of Phileas Fogg's race against time, writing with the aid of cardboard models of his characters which he moved over the surface of a map to ensure accuracy in times and places. According to his biographers, Verne completed *Around the World in Eighty Days* about November 1872, and it was in this same month that Thomas Cook — unaware of the great novel he had inspired — set of on his journey. The story was first serialised before book publication in *Le Temps* (trebling the circulation while it lasted) and was rapidly translated into English for British and American newspapers. It perhaps comes as no surprise to learn that there were many readers who believed Fogg's journey was actually taking place as they read about it, and there were several shipping lines and railways that approached Verne offering large sums of money if he would have his character travel safely and successfully by their transport and thereby provide excellent publicity! When the book was published the following year it was an immediate success and more copies — almost half a million — were sold in the French edition during its author's lifetime than any other. In this edited version of Thomas Cook's letters about his excursion which he sent back to the London *Times* it is interesting to find a number of similarities with Verne's novel: a clear indication of how carefully the author related his fiction to fact. (At the time of writing, the fastest recorded journey around the world is that achieved in November 1977 by a Pan American Boeing 747 carrying 150 passengers which flew a round trip from San Francisco, crossing both Poles, in 54 hours 7 minutes.)

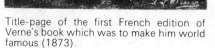

Title-page of the first French edition of Verne's book which was to make him world famous (1873).

A CIRCULAR TOUR
(*The Times*, November 27, 1872.)

We have been favoured by Mr Thomas Cook, the enterprising organiser of Tours, with the following interesting letter, the first, we hope, of a series. The letter is dated, San Francisco, October 31:

'Before leaving England on this greatest tour of my travelling life, I was pressed by many friends and by many inquiring correspondents to furnish particulars *en route* of any observations and experiences of countries through which we passed, and the various travelling and other accommodation essential to the comfort and convenience of a journey of over 25,000 miles. I promised to adopt the best medium of communicating with friends and the British public on these topics by writing to *The Times*, and on these grounds I ask your indulgence under a conviction that tours round the world will soon become a popular and instructive recreation to those who can command the necessary time and money.

'The season selected for this pioneering trip is, I believe, the very best that could have been chosen. Had we started one week earlier we might have visited from this point the wonderful Yosemite Valley and the big trees — one of the greatest of American attractions; but for all other points and countries we seem to be just right. We have crossed the great American Continent under the genial climate of the Indian Summer; we are at San Francisco at the commencement of the winter season, under the genial rays of a lovely and brilliant sun, the thermometer ranging at about 70 degrees, earth, air, sea and sky all alike attractive . . .

'Looking ahead, over the sea which seems worthy of the name Pacific, we are anticipating a good time in Japan and on its famed inland sea; in Hongkong and one or two places in China; in India in the very best month of the year (January); and then we shall be just right at Suez and Cairo for the Nile, and afterwards for Palestine, Turkey, Greece, Italy & etc.; all to be completed before the middle of May, when a detour may be made to the Vienna Exhibition before returning to London.

'My pioneering party is not large — eight today and maybe eleven when we sail tomorrow; but we represent, in pleasing harmony, England, Scotland, Russia, America and Greece, and it has been our pleasure to fall in with several English and American ladies and gentle-

men who bid fair to be pleasant companions. We also sail across the Pacific with a party of Japanese, who have spent five years in England, one of whom is a Prince of close relation to the ruling Mikado, and a second in succession to the throne of Japan. In a splendid and powerful steamer, and with such variety of companions, we anticipate a pleasant voyage of about 22 days across the Pacific.

'Our journey to this extreme point of the American continent has been all that could be reasonably desired. True, we had to contend against hard gales and strong head-winds in crossing the "Atlantic ferry". The excitement in the English Press just before we sailed from Liverpool about the accommodation for steerage passengers, led me to examine rather closely the ship's arrangements for the 778 of this class we had on board. I was permitted to go through the various departments of the ship, and I conversed with many of the most intelligent and rational-looking of the passengers, and was almost surprised to find how few were their complaints, notwithstanding the close

The original Phileas Fogg and his faithful manservant, Passepartout. (*Below*) A map from the Hetzel edition marking the route of the journey around the world.

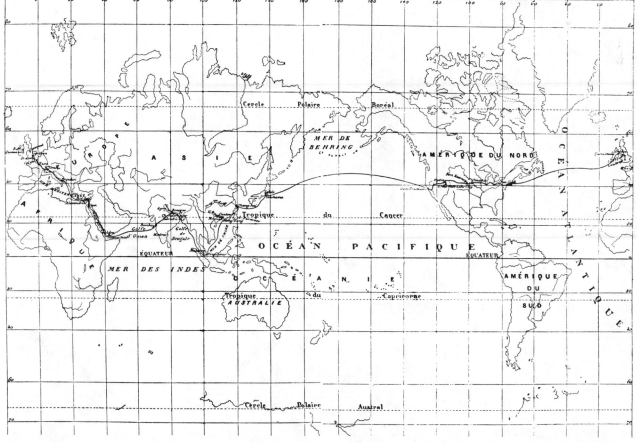

contact of 367 English men, women and children; 124 from Ireland, 184 Germans, 54 Swedes, 44 French and 3 Italians. With the exception of the beef being too salty and too hard, I scarcely heard a complaint, and the sleeping arrangements separated men from women, and married women and children from single women. When the whole "marched past" the examining medical officers at the New York quarantine station, I thought I never saw a more healthy or pleasant crowd of mixed nationalities, and considering the price paid for the 13 day passage and food (6 guineas), I could not but congratulate the White Star company on the facilities afforded for crossing the Atlantic. In the cabins there were 117 passengers — two thirds Americans — and the officers and crew numbered 146, thus making a total of 1,041 souls.

'Our stay at New York was limited to five days, quite sufficient for the general purpose of sight-seeing. The great railway trip from New York to San Francisco can be accomplished without difficulty in seven days and nights, but we broke the journey at the Falls of Niagara, at Detroit, at Chicago and at Salt Lake City. We selected the Erie Railway from half-a-dozen or more routes to Niagara and Chicago, and our ride in one of the Pulman's drawing room cars was most interesting.

'Our stay at Chicago for three days gave us ample time to see the phoenix-like restoration of this astonishing city, where there remain but faint traces of the devastation of twelve-month previous. Every public building, every church, every hotel and every mercantile establishment is completed, or in course of completion, on a larger scale than before the fire . . .

'From Chicago we took the Burlington route to Omaha, traversing the rich prairies of Illinois, crossing the Mississippi and the Missouri; from Omaha, still running over the prairies, and gradually ascending the long eastern slope towards the Rocky Mountains, until we reached the highest point of the road at Sherman, 8,242 feet above sea level. But it was difficult to realise the fact of this great elevation, the ascent from Omaha

(*Facing page*) The Red Indians massing around the train — a dramatic moment from *Around the World in Eighty Days*.

The stars of Mike Todd's 1956 epic version of *Around the World in Eighty Days*: David Niven, Shirley Maclaine, Cantinflas, Robert Newton.

The beautiful Princess Aouda who is rescued by Phileas Fogg — an engraving from the Hetzel edition.

being gradual most of the way. Prairie fires on all sides, antelopes, wolves and Indians kept us in a state of almost constant excitement. The Sioux tribe were evidently on the move to Southern quarters, as they were mounted in great force, on both sides of the line. They were supposed to be 500 at least, all mounted on very fine horses, gaudily dressed, and armed to the teeth. Had they been hostile they might have troubled us by closing their extended lines; but they gave evidence of friendship by cheers and actions, waving of caps and other signs of mirth.

'The total distance from New York the way we took was about 3,300 miles, and the detour from Ogden to Salt Lake City is about 37 miles. That detour we made and spent two days among the Mormons. All of my party were astonished at the magnitude and business characteristics of Salt Lake City, which is rapidly filling with a smart, Gentile population. The recently-discovered silver mines in the locality are attracting speculators and miners, and it will be difficult for Brigham Young and all his apostles and bishops to maintain the former exclusiveness of the city.

'I am afraid to add to the length of this letter, or I shall like to tell strangers to America of the peculiarities of the railways and the hotel systems of the United States. As it is arranged for the Pacific steamers going west and coming east to meet and transfer mails on the Pacific, if the sea does not dishonour its name. I may be able to add a few items to these hasty notes, with the view of showing the cost, conveniences and inconveniences of American travel.

'We have now completed about a fourth of our tour in distance. We have been coursing the "Far West" for about 6,300 miles. We have gone with the setting sun until my watch, which still adheres to Old Country time, points to 5 a.m. tomorrow, it being here but 9 p.m. I expect somewhere in the middle of the Pacific to lose a day, and then our next land will be that of the rising sun, travelling in the course

(*Top, left*) The shipwreck which spoils a holiday cruise but throws two young lovers together in *The Thompson Travel Agency* (1907).

(*Top, right*) *Salvage from the Cynthia* (1885) was the only book Verne wrote in collaboration – with a writer and radical socialist called André Laurie. The story is highlighted by a feat still to be achieved: the circumnavigation of the North Pole!

(*Left*) *The School for Crusoes* (1882) another Verne story inspired by his great admiration for Robinson Crusoe: although this time the castaway is specially staged to test survival techniques!

of which we will regain the losses of his decline in the west.'

* * *

From the Christmas Day issue of The Times, *December 25, 1872:*

COOK'S EXCURSION AROUND THE WORLD – The excursionists now making a tour round the world with Mr Thomas Cook, and who left San Francisco on the 1st of November last for Japan, arrived in Ceylon on the 20th inst. A telegram has been received from them to the following effect: 'Christmas cheer to all friends, including those in America. All well. Letters reach England January 20.'

Thomas Cook's next report appeared in The Times *of Thursday, January 23, 1873, and was written on board a Pacific Steamship and dated November 6. In this Cook describes in detail his impression of American hotel accommodation and rail travel which, in general, he approves of, although in many respects 'these institutions differ in their management and provisions from European accommodation'. He has, though, nothing but praise for the ship on which the party are sailing and concludes his letter:*

'In a week or ten days more we expect to reach the 180th degree of longitude, when London will be under our feet, and a day will mysteriously drop from the calendar. But this going round the world is a very easy and almost imperceptible business; there is no dificulty about it.'

* * *

The third letter appears in The Times *of March 12, 1873, and was written on board the ship* Hydaspes, *dated February 13. Cook is delighted with Japan and says 'the sail over the inland sea of Japan surpassed all my dreams'. China, though, is a big disappointment.*

'At Shanghai we visited the Old Chinese City, which presented a strong contrast to the Japanese cities we had just left. Narrow, filthy and offensive streets, choked and almost choking bazaars, pestering and festering beggars in every shape of hideous deformity; sights, sounds and smells all combined to cut short our promenade of the "native city" to which no one paid a second visit, and the chief part of our short stay at Shanghai was spent in the American, English or French concessions.'

The party later move on through Hongkong and Singapore taking in the sights and then sail to Ceylon which proves similarly interesting but uneventful. Their next destination is India.

When the group reach India, Thomas Cook reports in The Times *of March 24, 1873, he arranges for the party to travel in a special railway saloon carriage which can be attached and detached to engines as they choose. In this manner they travel for 2,300 miles. Cook is particularly appalled by sights such as those at the 'holy city of Benares' where 'we were conducted through five lines of idolatrous filth and obscurity, combining bull, peacock, monkey and other nameless objects of worship.' At the Ganges,*

Jules Verne satirised all those real-life travellers who subsequently tried to beat his round the world in eighty days, in the story *Claudius Bombarnac* (1893). In it, Baron Weisschnitzerdörfer tries to go round in 39 days, but makes such a mess of things he takes 187 days instead!

too, the susceptibilities of the party are also assailed: 'We saw crowds of bathers trying to wash away the "filth of the flesh"; others shaving the heads and washing dead bodies previous to laying them on the funeral piles, which were burning on the banks of the river. The whole of these heathen scenes were revolting in the extreme.' But it is in Bombay that Cook, a life-long abstainer from drink, is most horrified:

'In Bombay I saw in an evening ramble of observation, small shops with various coloured and variously labelled bottles arranged within reach of a priest of Bacchus; who sat cross-legged on a barrel or other elevation, waiting to dispense the liquid of seduction, and from his shrine, either behind or by a side passage, was a way to rooms above, from the windows of which lewd women were calling, singing and gesticulating to promenaders in the public street; and at the doors of some of the more fashionable resorts carriages were detained while their occupants were gone to worship at these double shrines of idolatry and vice. These parallel cases of the worship of Bacchus and Venus are alike destructive to native Indians in the one case and thoughtless Europeans in the other.'

In an interesting aside, Cook reveals that before leaving India for Egypt, he gives a lecture on abstinence to an audience of 500 British soldiers stationed at Akbar!

*   *   *

Thomas Cook's final letter appeared in The Times of May 27, 1873 when he describes how he is forced to leave the party and let them complete the final leg of their world trip on their own:

'On arrival at Suez, within a week's journey to London, my course was blockaded by intimation of an aggregate of about 75 tourists who had arrived or were en route for the East, depending on my services; and, leaving my round-the-world associates to go in any direction they desired, I tried my best to meet the exigencies of the busiest season ever known on the Nile and in Palestine . . .

'. . . I now close my round-the-world series of communications to The Times with an expression of gratitude for the prominence given to my flying notes of progress. Everywhere The Times and The Mail have heralded or notified this eight-month's run round and up and down the world, and, on the completion of the tour, on or about the sixth of May, I hope to be able to satisfy the demands of inquirers as to the practicability and expense of tours around the world'.

Thomas Cook

Round the world in 54 hours

San Francisco, Oct 31.—A Pan American World Airways Boeing 747 carrying 150 passengers landed here last night after flying round the world in a record 54 hours, 7 minutes.

The flight sliced more than eight hours off the old record of 62 hours 27 minutes set by a Boeing 707 cargo jet in 1965. The Pan Am jet travelled more than 26,000 miles and crossed the North and South Poles during the journey.

Twenty-two first class passengers had paid $3,333 (about £1,850) and the economy travellers $2,222 for the flight, which had been advertised as the chance of a lifetime. The airliner took off from San Francisco and flew via London, Cape Town and Auckland.

Mr Karl Mackling and his wife, Margaret, of Delray Beach, Florida, who are in their 60s, said they made the journey "because we're getting old, and we simply wanted to see the entire world in a short time."—Reuter.

A Musical Turn Round!

by George Robey

As a young man, Jules Verne's earliest attempts at writing were plays and sketches for the theatre, and although quite a few of his scripts were actually performed in Paris he enjoyed scant critical or financial success. Indeed, it was a cruel twist of fate that saw versions of his most famous books turned into stage productions by other hands and achieve enormous popularity. Fortunately, of course, Verne had a financial interest in these presentations and reaped rich rewards from the several long runs of versions of *Michael Strogoff* and *Around the World in Eighty Days* to name but two. The play about Strogoff, the 'courier of the czar' opened in 1880 to a great reception. The staging was particularly lavish and created such a sensation that it became the custom in France to describe anything fine as being *beau comme Strogoff*. The Russian costumes also turned Astrakhan and fur trimmings into the latest style for fashionable people and *poisson sauce tartare, caviar Ivan le Terrible, and glaces Berezina* were essentials on the menu of any Parisian restaurant that hoped to satisfy its clientele. After a time *Strogoff* was alternated with *Around the World in Eighty Days* at the Chatelet Theatre in Paris and the two productions ran there without a break for fifty years. The success of these plays was repeated wherever else they were staged, and in time they even attracted parodies of one sort or another. George Robey (1869–1954), 'The Prime Minister of Mirth' and perhaps the greatest of all British comics, always maintained that the revue, *Round in Fifty*, based on Verne's idea was the best production he ever appeared in, and this article describes what it was like for just one member of the theatrical profession who benefited from Jules Verne's genius.

(*Facing page*) Another moment from Mike Todd's *Around the World in Eighty Days* with Charles Boyer and Cantinflas studying one of Thomas Cook's first brochures; and a newspaper cutting of the latest record from *The Times*, November 1st 1977.

(*Above*) A caricature of Verne from *L'Eclipse*, November 1874, at the time of the opening of the play based on *Around the World in Eighty Days*.

The Revue, *Round in Fifty*, which opened in March 1922 was to prove another Hippodrome success. Right from the first night it went with a bang, and for months it crowded the house not only every night but at a matinée every day. Before the curtain rose on the first performance most people seemed to think the title had something to do with golf; but they soon discovered that it meant round the world in fifty days, and was an up-to-date version of Jules Verne's famous romance of our boyhood's years, *Round the World in Eighty Days*. Written by Sax Rohmer, in collaboration with Julian and Lauri Wylie, and set to music by James W. Tate just before his death and by Herman Finck, it showed Phileas (here called Phineas) Fogg making his famous wager and winning it. It took the audience from the Gridiron Club, London, to scenes in Boulogne, Brindisi, Hong-Kong, San Francisco, New York, Caliornia, Portsmouth, and so back to London and victory. There were some beautiful scenes in it, notably a white and silver Chinese ballet under white pagodas and a crimson sky, and a lovely orange grove in California, turning from day to night, with a steamer all lit up crossing a lake in the background, and the oranges turning into balls of fire. There was also as smart a quick-change scene as I ever saw, from an elaborate and dissolute cabaret interior to a grim Pussyfoot missionary revival meeting! The change was made in a few seconds, and it brought the house down every time.

My part was that of old Fogg's spendthrift son, Phil (you will remember he was the valet, Passepartout, in the novel). It was a lovely part from beginning to end. One of Phil's worries on his travels was that he had left a taxi-cab ticking for him in London, and from time to time he agonisedly wondered what its dial was registering. 'Fifty days,' I soliloquised, 'fifty days of twenty-four hours each, at tuppence a tick — how much change will there be for me out of a pound-note when I get back?' In the scene of the 'Frisco Cabaret I tried to win at the tables, and when all my money was gone, I started investing garment after garment till at last I entered wearing nothing but a bathing costume, boots and socks, and a top hat! In this plight, Renée Reel, in the part of my telephone-girl sweetheart, Penelope, came up and offered me a loan of money. 'No,' I said firmly, 'I could not accept a loan from a woman — especially a lady!' *Punch* seemed to like that episode, for it put a drawing

From *Punch*, March 22nd 1922.

of me in it in the middle of a page. In another scene I was a convict in Sing-Sing prison, where a 'charity entertainment' of songs, recitations and conjuring was being given to the 'pore prisoners' by well-meaning but wildly incapable people, and the convicts were finding it worse than the treadmill! I remember the whole scene as a hit from beginning to end. After one of the most awful contributions of the awful amateurs I ejaculated in loud despair, 'Lor' luv a duck! An' they 'ung Crippen!' and I still seem to hear the roar of the audience that followed.

In another scene a Singing Pullet figured. 'You pullet and it sings!' was the joke. In another I had an 'adopted elephant', which trumpeted loudly 'off' when I was soliloquising. At last, in desperation, I rushed from the stage, and returned in a few moments staggering under the weight of two huge ivory tusks. 'I'll teach elephants to argue!' I exclaimed. And in one scene how the critics bellowed in mirth when I recklessly cried, 'Who cares what the critics say!' As it happened, they had none but nice things to say

next day. The scene in the Pussyfoot chapel where I explained what a reprobate I had been in my alcoholic past, and led the chorus in temperance hymns also seemed to give the audience great comfort; and after one of my songs I quite electrified the house by giving a step dance which, as several critics remarked, showed I could twiddle my feet with the best of them, and finishing up with a complete cart-wheel, in spite of my fifty years. The reader will, I hope, excuse all this about myself, but it really was a jolly part, and I did enjoy it.

Renée Reel looked and acted gaily as Penelope, and the company also included the cousins, Wallace and Barry Lupino, Alex Kellaway, Jean Allistone and Ruth French with the 'Hippodrome Eight' in the principal dances. The production went as smooth as butter on the first night, for we had had a preliminary week with it at Cardiff; and the melodies of Tate and of Finck were real ones that soothe and charm, not the nigger-music kind of stuff that could never make anyone but a nit-wit happy. In

fact, the show was classified on the programme as "a musical adventure", and musical it *was*. And presently it became still more so when Helen Gilliland, who had done such dainty work in Gilbert and Sullivan opera, came into the cast as the lady journalist, Jill Carey, and warbled mellifluously in the 'Romance of the Tea-leaves', and the gorgeously coloured Californian scenes.

I only heard of one soul who couldn't abide *Round in Fifty*. He came one afternoon to see it, and afterwards had to be helped into a cab by the whole front-door staff. When he got home he wrote a letter to his pet paper and sent me a copy. Part of it ran as follows:—

Why do people laugh at Robey? When in this revue he exclaims to a fair temptress: 'It is women like you that make men like me like women like you' the audience rocked. When strolling into a scene purporting to represent a cabaret in San Francisco he beamingly remarked 'So this is Genoa!' they nearly fell out of their

seats. When he helplessly asked the audience 'Am I mad, or is it only insanity?' they bellowed like the bull of Basan. And when, shut up in a prison cell and clad in convict garb he murmured sadly 'All this is so new to me!' I thought the laughter would never end. Why all this?

It does seem odd, doesn't it? But who can compass the scope of the human mind? What does the great Welsh poet say on this very subject? Permit me to quote that memorable quatrain:—

Uwch y ser hoenwych, siriol –
   Haul ydyw
  Y gwyliedydd nefol;
Hwythau, fel gronynan'n ol
   O dano, yn gadwynol.

There you have it! Yet how few people know those profound and trenchant lines! And how fewer still are aware that the name of their author was — John L. Toole!

Altogether I think *Round in Fifty* was the best revue I ever took part in. To begin with, it had a really good plot that kept the audience excited from

(*Facing page and above*) Three of the illustrations from the novel *Michael Strogoff – Courier to the Czar* (1876) which became an even bigger success as a stage play.

Akim Tamiroff in the 1937 version of *Michael Strogoff* – and the same scene moments later, but in a version of the film made a quarter of a century later starring Curt Jurgens.

start to finish. Then it introduced the cinematograph (which was more of a novelty some years ago than it is to-day) in a most interesting way. The gradual approach of an Atlantic liner which I was trying to catch up in a motor launch was most effective, and always got thunderous applause. So also did the race along the Portsmouth road, which was won just in time to secure the wager, thanks to the unexpected coming in of winter time, giving an extra hour. And, last but not least, the show was produced in his very best style by Julian Wylie, one of the ablest fashioners of revue and pantomime in the country, always introducing novelties, one of the easiest men to work with, and also one of the most appreciative.

(*Below*) *Keraban the Inflexible* (1883) was another novel set in Asia which Verne hoped would repeat the success of *Michael Strogoff* both as a book and stage play. Unfortunately, it did neither.

A PLUNGE INTO SPACE

Jules Verne not only kept himself fully informed of all new scientific developments by careful reading of the newspaper and magazines, but was also very interested in the work of other writers exploiting the vein he had opened. In 1890 a popular British writer of fiction, Robert Cromie, wrote an interplanetary adventure entitled *A Plunge Into Space* and dedicated it to Verne, 'To whom I am indebted for many delightful and marvellous excursions — notably, a voyage from the earth to the moon, a trip twenty thousand leagues under the sea and a journey round the world in eighty days — and who, in return, has now courteously consented to accompany me to the planet Mars, at the rate of fifty thousand miles a minute.' When he read the book, Verne was intrigued by the originality of the story — the space vessel is the first of its kind to be globular in shape — and provided an introduction (the only one he is known to have done) for the second edition which appeared a year later. He also took the opportunity of expressing his appreciation to this enthusiastic readers across the Channel.

TO MY ENGLISH READERS

Especially to those who have followed me on my far journeys, I have pleasure in introducing a pupil. With him I have just made a voyage, weird and wild. He pointed out many interesting things on the way. For myself, I should perhaps have preferred more details, more facts and figures in connection with the stupendous phenomena we encountered. But the pace at which we travelled was not favourable to minute inquiry — one does not reckon the wavelets when one estimates the strength of the tides.

With this brief introduction I must leave the voyage in the Steel Globe to those who choose to make it. Certainly, it is a 'terrible venture', but they need not fear; their guide is skilful and bold. They may trust themselves in his hands. He will serve them well.

Jules Verne,
Amiens.

From *Strand Magazine*, December 1895.

An Express of the Future

FROM THE FRENCH OF JULES VERNE.

"TAKE care!" cried my conductor, "there's a step!"

Safely descending the step thus indicated to me, I entered a vast room, illuminated by blinding electric reflectors, the sound of our feet alone breaking the solitude and silence of the place.

Where was I? What had I come there to do? Who was my mysterious guide? Questions unanswered. A long walk in the night, iron doors opened and reclosed with a clang, stairs descending, it seemed to me, deep into the earth—that is all I could remember. I had, however, no time for thinking.

"No doubt you are asking yourself who I am?" said my guide: "Colonel Pierce, at your service. Where are you? In America, at Boston—in a station."

"A station?"

"Yes, the starting-point of the 'Boston to Liverpool Pneumatic Tubes Company.'"

And, with an explanatory gesture, the Colonel pointed out to me two long iron cylinders, about a mètre and a half in diameter, lying upon the ground a few paces off.

I looked at these two cylinders, ending on the right in a mass of masonry, and closed on the left with heavy metallic caps, from which a cluster of tubes were carried up to the roof; and suddenly I comprehended the purpose of all this.

Had I not, a short time before, read, in an American newspaper, an article describing this extraordinary project for linking Europe with the New World by means of two gigantic submarines tubes? An inventor had claimed to have accomplished the task; and that inventor, Colonel Pierce, I had before me.

In thought I realized the newspaper article.

Complaisantly the journalist entered into the details of the enterprise. He stated that more than 3,000 miles of iron tubes, weighing over 13,000,000 tons, were required, with the number of ships necessary, for the transport of this material—200 ships of 2,000 tons, each making thirty-three voyages. He described this Armada of science bearing the steel to two special vessels, on board of which the ends of the tubes were joined to each other, and incased in a triple netting of iron, the whole covered with a resinous preparation to preserve it from the action of the sea-water.

Coming at once to the question of working, he filled the tubes—transformed into a sort of pea-shooter of interminable length—with a series of carriages, to be carried with their travellers by powerful currents of air, in the same way that despatches are conveyed pneumatically round Paris.

A parallel with the railways closed the article, and the author enumerated with enthusiasm the advantages of the new and audacious system. According to him, there would be, in passing through these tubes, a suppression of all nervous trepidation, thanks to the interior surface being of finely polished steel; equality of temperature secured

THE PNEUMATIC TUBES.

by means of currents of air, by which the heat could be modified according to the seasons; incredibly low fares, owing to the cheapness of construction and working expenses—forgetting, or waving aside, all considerations of the question of gravitation and of wear and tear.

All that now came back to my mind.

So, then, this "Utopia" had become a reality, and these two cylinders of iron at my feet passed thence under the Atlantic and reached to the coast of England!

In spite of the evidence, I could not bring myself to believe in the thing having been done. That the tubes had been laid I could not doubt; but that men could travel by this route—never!

"Was it not impossible even to obtain a current of air of that length?"—I expressed that opinion aloud.

"Quite easy, on the contrary!" protested Colonel Pierce; "to obtain it, all that is required is a great number of steam fans similar to those used in blast furnaces. The air is driven by them with a force which is practically unlimited, propelling it at the speed of 1,800 kilomètres an hour—almost that of a cannon-ball!—so that our carriages with their travellers, in the space of two hours and forty minutes, accomplish the journey between Boston and Liverpool."

"Eighteen hundred kilomètres an hour!" I exclaimed.

"Not one less. And what extraordinary consequences arise from such a rate of speed!

The time at Liverpool being four hours and forty minutes in advance of ours, a traveller starting from Boston at nine o'clock in the morning, arrives in England at 3.53 in the afternoon. Isn't that a journey quickly made? In another sense, on the contrary, our trains, in this latitude, gain over the sun more than 900 kilomètres an hour, beating that planet hand over hand: quitting Liverpool at noon, for example, the traveller will reach the station where we now are at thirty-four minutes past nine in the morning—that is to say, earlier than he started! Ha! ha! I don't think one can travel quicker than *that!*"

I did not know what to think. Was I talking with a madman?—or must I credit these fabulous theories, in spite of the objections which rose in my mind?

"Very well, so be it!" I said. "I will admit that travellers may take this madbrained route, and that you can obtain this incredible speed. But, when you have got this speed, how do you check it? When you come to a stop, everything must be shattered to pieces!"

"Not at all," replied the Colonel, shrugging his shoulders. "Between our tubes—one for the out, the other for the home journey—consequently worked by currents going in opposite directions—a communication exists at every joint. When a train is approaching, an electric spark advertises us of the fact; left to itself, the train would continue its course by reason of the speed it had acquired; but, simply by the turning of a handle, we are able to let in the opposing current of compressed air from the parallel tube, and, little by little, reduce to nothing the final shock or stopping. But what is the use of all these explanations? Would not a trial be a hundred times better?"

And, without waiting for an answer to his questions, the Colonel pulled sharply a bright brass knob projecting from the side of one of the tubes: a panel slid smoothly in its grooves, and in the opening left by its removal I perceived a row of seats, on each of which two persons might sit comfortably side by side.

"The carriage!" exclaimed the Colonel. "Come in."

I followed him without offering any objection, and the panel immediately slid back into its place.

By the light of an electric lamp in the roof I carefully examined the carriage I was in.

Nothing could be more simple: a long cylinder, comfortably upholstered, along which some fifty arm-chairs, in

INSIDE THE CAR.

pairs, were ranged in twenty-five parallel ranks. At either end a valve regulated the atmospheric pressure, that at the farther end allowing breathable air to enter the carriage, that in front allowing for the discharge of any excess beyond a normal pressure.

After spending a few moments on this examination, I became impatient.

"Well," I said, "are we not going to start?"

"Going to start?" cried the Colonel. "We *have* started!"

Started—like that—without the least jerk, was it possible? I listened attentively, trying to detect a sound of some kind that might have guided me.

If we had really started—if the Colonel had not deceived me in talking of a speed of eighteen hundred kilomètres an hour—we must already be far from any land, under the sea; above our heads the huge, foam-crested waves; even at that moment, perhaps—taking it for a monstrous sea-serpent of an unknown kind—whales were battering with their powerful tails our long, iron prison!

But I heard nothing but a dull rumble, produced, no doubt, by the passage of our carriage, and, plunged in boundless astonishment, unable to believe in the reality of all that had happened to me, I sat silently, allowing the time to pass.

At the end of about an hour, a sense of freshness upon my forehead suddenly aroused me from the torpor into which I had sunk by degrees.

I raised my hand to my brow: it was moist.

Moist! Why was that? Had the tube burst under pressure of the waters—a pressure which could not but be formidable, since it increases at the rate of "an atmosphere" every ten mètres of depth? Had the ocean broken in upon us?

Fear seized upon me. Terrified, I tried to call out—and—and I found myself in my garden, generously sprinkled by a driving rain, the big drops of which had awakened me. I had simply fallen asleep while reading the article devoted by an American journalist to the fantastic projects of Colonel Pierce—who, also, I much fear, has only dreamed.

THE FUTURE FOR WOMEN

An Address by Jules Verne

One development which Jules Verne clearly did not envisage — or perhaps did not want to see — was women's liberation. When, in July 1893, he was invited to deliver an address at the local *Lycée de Jeunes Filles* in Amiens, he went to considerable pains to stress to his young listeners that their futures lay as dutiful wives and that all their education should be dedicated to this end. He also urged them against taking undue exercise — cycling and skating in particular! Perhaps the only element that saves this speech from being the statement of a wholehearted chauvinist is Verne's approval of the idea of women speakers at prize-giving ceremonies and the suggestion that he might even support a woman president! This marks the first publication of the speech and the translation has been specially prepared by I. O. Evans. (In this context it is interesting to note that sex rarely appears in Verne stories, and female heroines are only to be found in a few of his books like *A Family Without A Name* (1889), *Mistress Branican* (1891), *The Golden Volcano* (1906) and *The Barsac Mission* (1920).

Imagine if you will, ladies, the position an elderly story-teller like me finds himself in today. A man whose only care is to make up yarns more or less extraordinary by giving vent to a boundless imagination — an imagination which would be quite out of place here! So, naturally, I have long pondered and racked my brains to extract from them some sort of speech in which ideas would be replaced by words painfully stitched together. So prepare yourselves!

You will not be angry with me, I trust, if, remembering the sheer impossibility of rivalling my honourable predecessors on this platform, I have made the heroic resolution to vary their method, and when I come here to speak . . . simply not to say anything, after the style of an art which in our time has been brought to perfection.

Hadjine, the heroine of *The Archipelago on Fire* (1884) who devotes herself to spending the fortune her father amassed dishonestly in alleviating all the evil he did. (*Opposite*) Helena Glenarven who helps lead the search for a missing sea captain in *Among The Cannibals* one of the three volumes in the odyssey *A Voyage Round The World* (1868).

JULES
VERNE

The truth is that there is a gap in the programme of secondary education. Fortunately, may I say, they are talking of filling it, by creating in the *lycées* and the colleges a special class for prize-giving speeches! That's a praise-worthy idea, but I don't know when it will be put into effect. It will be essential, however, if anyone wishes to vary the general run of these time-honoured addresses, too often given up to the usual banalities. Then never again shall we hear those traditional words:

'I am afraid I haven't got the requisite qualities ... Excuse my confusion in the presence of this large audience ... It is rash of me to attempt such a thing ... A voice more authoritative than mine ...'

No, the orator will select from his old exercise-books such and such a

speech appropriate for such and such a public; and for my part if that class had existed in the time long past when I went to school, and if I had won the first prize, I should not have been as embarrassed as I am today.

Well, to get to the point! I do not feel any embarrassment – not even the most fearsome of all those inherent in my position – the embarrassment of entering into competition with the eminent personnages whom you have already heard. Here, before my time, the charmers have said excellent things excellently well ... Never mind! I am not afraid of comparison with them, for the very good reason that I lack the presumption to seek to vie with them. I am resigned to following a different path to reach the moment when this over-fantastic reading will give place to the far more attractive reading of the prize-list. Yes, attractive for you, for your parents, for your friends, especially when the names of the prize-winners, Mademoiselle X . . ., Mademoiselle Y, . . ., Mademoiselle Z . . ., are accompanied by the flattering comment, mentioned twice, four times, six times, ten times!

So, faithful to this system, I shall take care not, as the former orators have done, to praise your schoolmistresses – no, not even you *Directrice* Madame Bertrand. I shall not announce that she has succeeded in putting into practice the high promises she made in the first session of 1885.

I shall not repeat that her only thought is to instruct you, that, putting aside the questions which might divide you, her only aim is to produce hearts full of love for *la patrie française*, and – to use the words spoken by the Minister for Public Instruction in a recent address at the opening of the *Lycée de Jeunes* Filles at Puy – 'to produce courageous and disinterested women who will place their souls, their knowledge, and their virtue at the service of national greatness'.

Neither will I say that the University does not seek to produce savants in us or jugglers of the algebraical *x*, still less to transform its pupils into the blue-stockings of every hue, from the police-blue which forms the emblem of the literary ladies to the azure which symbolises the Eratos, the Caliopes and the Polyhymnias of modern poetry.

Cannibalism was the theme of *The Survivors of the Chancellor* (1875) which has been described as the grimmest story Verne ever wrote.
(*Top*) One of the passengers on the drifting raft hangs himself in despair, while (*left*) another is about to sacrifice his hands so the rest may have something to eat.

And, indeed, for a woman — it cannot be repeated too often — isn't it better to inspire verses than to make them? So your education has been arranged very judiciously, and, if a few of you are to study law or medicine in order to wear the neckbands of the lawyers or to wield the scalpel of the lady-doctor, they will be in the minority. The teaching of your mistresses will gradually prepare you for the parts you are to play. Thanks to them, the control of a family which will be placed in your hands will lead you into the true way in which a woman should exert her social influence. 'The woman always know where to find Providence' said Victor Hugo and I am certain that when you leave school, you will know where to find it, when there is some good to do, some sorrow to console, some misfortune to overcome.

And what I am saying to the young ladies will apply no less to the little girls. Indeed, are there any little girls? . . . No, according to a witty humorist who is among my friends, there are only smaller women, and I gladly agree with him.

So, big and little alike, take care not to go astray when traversing the scientific domain. Do not plunge too deeply into 'science, the magnificent gulf', to use the expression of the great poet, in which man sometimes loses his way. Do not forsake anything of the duties of your sex. As you are among the privileged of this world, hang on to your privileges.

And may I be allowed to protest against the sally of that sorry jester, quoted even here in a very witty talk by Monsieur Mollard, who dared to assert: 'In woman, we can already feel the Creator's weariness!' If woman, did not appear until after man, it is because the Creator wished first to try His hand, to perfect Himself for His last and fairest creation, by following that Law of Nature which demands progress. Women must therefore congratulate themselves on being in the heart of a considerate society and must disdainfully repulse the completely absurd demands which are never tired of seeking to produce shockheaded politicianesses.

What is one to think of those who try to throw themselves into the social battles at the time when the finest citizens are overwhelmed with insults; who claim to rush into business tumults at a time when so many risks and so many disappointments are piling up; who want to jostle one another to make their way, at a time when there is nothing to collect but bruises? You would do better to direct your

aptitudes in bringing happiness to the hearth and home. Satisfy yourselves with being gracious when the men are uncouth, beautiful when they are ugly, gentle when they are coarse, good when they are bad, angels when they are devils! Be content with the part which is assigned to you.

I find that quite enviable. You live at the centre of attention and homage. Everywhere you are in the front row and the first tier — at dinner the first to be served; at the dance the first to be invited; in conversation the first to be heard; in ceremonies the first to take the best places. And do not all of us feel honoured that you deign to accept our attentions, our courtesy, our deference . . . and our hearts? Heavens, how I have longed to be a woman — at least for a few years!

An advertisement from *The Bookseller* of Christmas 1892, for Verne's intrepid *Mistress Branican* who leads an expedition into central Australia where they have many exciting adventures.

I know that it is for a man to defend *La Patrie*, to rush to her threatened frontier, to pour out his blood in her service! This is a noble duty in which no patriot has ever failed. But, first, does it not seem that Continental wars are getting less frequent? And, anyhow, even in these troublous times, have you not your own generous part to play? And to serve under the Red Cross Flag and that of the Women of France, is not that to serve under the French flag itself?

So do not envy us at all! Sweet little girls, seek to become charming young ladies. Young ladies, seek to become accomplished women. Women, seek

to become mothers of families. Mothers of families, seek to become grandmothers crowned with white hair. That crown becomes you more than our premature baldness, denuding our skulls before we grow old.

But on consulting your programme, I was seized by a very natural dread. Heavens, young Lycéans, what you've got to learn during your five years at the Lycée! What trees of science are growing in your garden, trees which, I hope will never bear withered fruit! What complicated instruction! It includes French language and literature, ancient literature, ethics, living languages — English and German — foreign literature, geography, history, cosmography, common law, psychology, economy — not political, I hasten to admit, but domestic — physics, general chemistry, drawing, music, gymnastics, the cutting and making of clothes, etc.

I assure you that if I had to pass an exam in half of these matters, the marks I should obtain would be nothing short of derisory — not even in cutting and making. On the whole, that is all very well; but, believe me, that your head, a little borne down by all these fine things, will not outweigh the other scale-pan, the one which contains your heart. Try, later on, to find some useful application for all that you've learned.

What, even Latin, you will say to me, you advice-monger, for we're learning Latin! We have two professors from the boys' Lycée, a Fellow of the University, a master of arts, MM Lenci and Helot. I know that, and I cannot but congratulate these honourable professors on teaching you that admirable tongue spoken by the ladies of Ancient Rome as they chastely spun their wool. Hurrah for *rosa the rose, liber Petri, amo Deum,* and the rule of *que* suppressed.

May the study of the venerable Lhomond help you to grasp the origin and the exact meaning of many of the words of our no less admirable French language. I hope, moreover, that your instructress in cooking — or, I should say, domestic economy — will not be satisfied with initiating you into the arts of the pastrycook or the confectioner but will inculcate you with the principles of culinary Latin. May you, when you leave the course in general chemistry, know how to make a *pot au feu* according to the rules, and to combine in the correct proportions the elements of mutton-broth, far better than the ambrosia of Olympus, the recipe for which has never been discovered, in spite of the researches of archaeologists as tenacious as they

A young girl disguised as a boy who is searching for her lost father is the theme of *Le Superbe Orénoque* (1898).

are fond of good living!

As for gymnastics, ladies, steer clear of any excess. Exercises appropriate to your taste, to your strength, nothing could profit you more — like hoops, skipping rope, badminton, playing touch, in which we see the competitors of the primary schools showing such ardour when *M. le Maire* invites us to preside at their competitive games. But no over-extertion in these sports, for it is against this that you must especially be on the watch.

No athletic sports, and, above all, no cycling! Leave the pedals to men in a hurry. Don't mix up with a complicated system of gearing elegance of your gait, and never put screeching rollerskates on your little feet, which ought to be quite enough for you — even to run into Providence!

Now here I am at the end of my mandate, and it is not without a sort of apprehension that I think of my successor for next year. Oh, it's not that I'm presumptuous enough to think that I've made the position more difficult for him; but I cannot possibly imagine what else is left for him to say, assuming that the prize-giving speech won't be suppressed next year.

Still if this much-to-be-desired policy isn't adopted there may be some way of restoring new life to these sessions, to pour into another mould — finer, more delicate, more artistic — these speeches indispensable to these ceremonies at the University. This course I find indicated in a discourse made in 1890, and I'm much in favour of trying it. At that time Monsieur Dauphin said with as much wit as relevance, 'The men will have enough

regard for themselves and good grace to let themselves be dethroned in this place by the women and to beg one of them to preside over this prize-giving.' And on the following year, in a charming speech, Monsieur Allain Targe, Prefect of the Somme, declared himself an absolute partisan of a feminine Presidency.

Here is a practical idea, if ever there was one, and whose adoption should be demanded without delay! If the Ministry of Public Instruction is well-advised, he will consult the Rector of the Academy on this point. Then these two lofty functionaries will make haste to replace the harsh masculine voice by one of those feminine voices which nature has so melodiously set an octave higher.

In a country where everything ends, no longer in songs, as in that splendid time which Beaumarchais regrets so much, but in countless interpellations, men, it must be admitted, are at the end of their strength, so freely do they exhaust themselves in harangues, in counsel's addresses, toasts of all kinds and for all occasions. Words worn out by too frequent a use, creak abominably between our lips. And I — I who speak, ladies, I shall run out of breath if I have to fill up the regulation half-hour up to the last minute!

With a president in a robe — I mean a bell-shaped robe, with puffed sleeves, an empire corsage, and not the black robe of the professor or the red robe of the magistrate — the attractions of our sessions will be magnificently increased. The address would be gracious, witty, elegant, suggestive, up-to-date, and be assured that it would finish . . . although it come from a feminine mouth.

Jane and Edith who seek adventure in the Klondike find more than they bargained for in *The Golden Volcano* (1906).

The brave young women who first saves from death and then falls in love with the adventurer, *Clovis Dardentor* (1896).

I have completed my task, ladies. Brief as I have forced myself to be, I have said quite enough for your taste. A very witty humorist who was asked if he had found any interest in an infant prodigy who had just played an endless tune on the piano, replied:

'She interested me more when she began'.

'And why?'

'Because she was younger!'

I would like to think I hadn't been talking so long . . . long enough to earn me a disagreeable reply. No doubt I was younger when I began and that may have made me more interesting? But I don't think that my hairs have turned white since I began to speak. As for you, Ladies, even when I look hard at you, I scarcely think that you've reached the limits of extreme old age.

So I flatter myself I have stayed to some degree acceptable. Anyhow, you have known how to make my task easier by listening to me with so much goodwill and if I had the right to add a suggestion to your prize-list I would bestow to all of you, *ex-oequo*, large and small, a prize for long-continued attention.

So, ladies, applaud, applaud as enthusiastically as you like, not to congratulate me on what I've said, but to show your liveliest satisfaction . . . because I've finished saying it.

(*Facing page*) Ursula Andress the beautiful and brave heroine of *The Southern Star Mystery*, the film based on Verne's novel of the search for the biggest and finest diamond in the world which has been stolen. The inset illustration is from the first English publication of the novel under the title, *The Vanished Diamond* (1884).

JULES VERNE REVISITED

by Robert H. Sherard

Despite the passing years, and the dawning of the Twentieth Century, new works by the ageing Jules Verne continued to appear year in and year out without any sign of diminishing. Although he was actually writing less because of ill-health and failing eyesight, he had managed to stock-pile manuscripts over the years to keep up his commitment to Hetzel of two books per year. But the incredible output, combined with the author's reclusive life, gave rise to a rumour which spread rapidly that Verne was no longer himself writing the books and that they were the product of a group of literary hacks referred to as 'Jules Verne et Cie'. As always Verne himself remained indifferent to such allegations, until finally exasperated friends began urging him to allow a few important journalists to visit Amiens and by seeing him at work squash the rumours and thereby safeguard his reputation. Somewhat reluctantly, Verne agreed, and one of the most noted British journalists, Robert H. Sherard, called on him in the autumn of 1903. Sherard had visited Verne previously with Nellie Bly, an American journalist, working for the *New York World* who made the first attempt to beat the round-the-world record of 80 days. In 1889–90 she reduced the time to 72 days, 6 hours, 11 minutes and 14 seconds, and during her route across France stopped off to pay her respects to Verne. Sherard's report of his visit to the ageing author appeared in the now defunct, *T.P.'s Weekly* of October 9, 1903.

For months past evil, recurrent rumours have alarmed the world-wide constituency of Jules Verne. He was said to have become quite blind. We knew that to him to live is to work, albeit a very, very old man, and the pity of the situation seemed great.

Let me say at once that things are not so bad with him as one had feared. If one eye is completely gone, he can still see a little with the other.

'It is cataract in my right eye,' he said to me this morning in the drawing-room of his house at 44, Boulevard de Longueville, in grey and level Amiens. 'But the other eye is still fairly good. I do not want to risk an operation as long as I can see enough to do the little work, the little writing, the little reading, that I can still do, for remember, sir, that I am a very old man now, past seventy-six. Since the report of my blindness got about the sym-

pathies of the world have been awakened. I have received numerous letters from all parts. Many people have sent me prescriptions for cataract,

Jules Verne and his wife, Honorine, pictured at their home.

(*Above*) *Un Drame en Livonie* (1904) a detective story which Verne wrote as a result of his admiration for Poe.

(*Right*) Wil Mitz the schoolboy hero who defeats the dastardly pirate, Harry Markel in *Bourses de Voyage* (1903).

marvellous remedies. They tell me not to allow any operation to be performed; that these remedies of theirs will cure me without danger. It is very kind of them. I have been much touched, but, I know, of course, that an operation is the only cure.'

A comfortable home-life

I had not seen Jules Verne for nearly fourteen years. The last occasion on which I was with him was when I brought Nellie Bly to his house during her famous record-beating scamper round the world. Yet I did not find him as aged as I had feared. He looked plump and comfortable in his black alpaca suit, and his beautiful face, set in hair and beard that was white, was serene and animated in turn. His fine eyes in no way betrayed by their appearance the lurking mischief.

He is now living in a smaller house, but it is opulent and *cossu*, and a comfortable home life surrounds him.

Whenever, in our conversation, he admitted some defeat by circumstance and the inevitable law of Nature, he made haste, in his native cheerfulness, to find some compensation for it.

Years ahead of the publishers

'Although I can work very little now – terribly little as compared to former days – I am years ahead of the printing-press. My latest book of the series of *Extraordinary Voyages* is to be published shortly, under the title of *Bourses de Voyage* – there are thirteen complete manuscripts of the same series ready for the press. As you know, I publish two volumes a year, which appear first as serials in the *Magasin de Récréation*, of which I was one of the founders. I am now working on my new story, which will not be wanted by the printers till about 1910. *J'ai beaucop d'avance*, and so it does not matter so much that I have to work slowly, very slowly. I get up as usual at six in the morning and I am at my writing-table till 11 a.m. In the afternoon, as I always did, I go to the reading-room of the *Société Industrielle* and read as much as my eyes allow me to read.'

Stories come but titles linger

'I cannot say what is the title of the book I am writing. *Je n'en sais rien.* Nor have I any titles for the thirteen other stories which are waiting their turn. All I can say about the latest work is that it deals with *Un Drame en Livonée*, and that I have introduced into it . . . well, no, you mustn't print that, or some other writer may take my idea.'

It was inevitable, as Jules Verne remarked, that I should speak to him about H. G. Wells.

'*Je pensais bien que vous alliez me demander cela*,' he said. 'His books were sent to me, and I have read them. It is very curious, and, I will add, very English. But I do not see the possibility of comparison between his work and mine. We do not proceed in the same manner. It occurs to me that his stories do not repose on very scientific bases. No, there is no *rapport* between his work and mine. I make use of physics. He invents. I go to the moon in a cannon-ball, discharged from a cannon. Here there is no invention. He goes to Mars in an airship, which he constructs of a metal which does away with the law of gravitation. *Ca c'est*

très joli,' cried Monsieur Verne in an animated way, 'but show me this metal. Let him produce it.'

Fiction as fact

It was inevitable also that I should refer to the fact that many of his inventions in fiction have become inventions in fact. Here the amiable Madame Verne concurred with me.

'People are kind enough to say so,' said Jules Verne. 'It is flattering, but as a fact it is not true.'

'But come, Jules,' said Madame Verne, 'and your submarines?'

'*Acun rapport,*' said Verne, waving the flattery aside.

'*Mais si.*'

'*Mais non.* The Italians had invented submarine boats sixty years before I created Nemo and his boat. There is no connection between my boat and those now existing. These latter are worked by mechanical means. My hero, Nemo, being a misanthropist, and wishing to have nothing to do with the land, gets his motive force, electricity, from the sea. There is scientific basis for that, for the sea contains stores of electric force, just as the earth does. But how to get at this force has never been discovered, and so I have invented nothing.'

Names in fiction

We touched on the subject of the importance of names in fiction.

'I do attach certain importance to them' he said, 'and when I found "Fogg" I was very pleased and proud. And it was very popular. It was considered a real *trouvaille.* And yet Fogg – Fogg – that means nothing but *brouillard.* But it was especially the Phileas that gave such value to the creation. Yes, there is importance in names. Look at the wonderful god-fatherships of Balzac.'

We had begun to talk in the opulent drawing-rooms downstairs, two salons en suite with the dining-room beyond, and outside a garden full of flowers, on which the sun was shining. Opulent rooms, with heavy velvet hangings, great clocks and mirrors, full-length portraits, Venetian glass, and rarest bric-á-brac. It was natural that in time we should ascend the two flights of stairs to the workrooms of the man of letters.

Workrooms: one for reading, where the bulk of the library is; one for writing, where the little table is and the pen and ink is.

No luxury

All very simple here. No luxury. Maps on the wall, and in the writing-room a few pictures, including a watercolour of the *Saint Michel,* the yacht in which, in the free and sunny days of restless youth, Jules Verne

Jules Verne nursed a passion for the circus throughout his life, and his novel *César Cascabel* (1890) concerns the adventures of a family of jugglers who travel eventfully throughout America and Russia performing their act.

ranged the world's water.

We had been talking just then of *le reportage Américain,* and to keep in the note, I remarked, 'There must be at least three yards of them!'

He laughed heartily and made as if to measure the shelf.

'Oh, yes,' he said, 'I have written at least three yards. And look at all those yards of translation. English, French, Danish, Italian, all the tongues.'

Eight long shelves were filled with books with the same name on every cover.

In the inner room, where it is twilight, stands against the window the little deal table on which nearly all the books have been penned. A bomb on the window-sill serves as a paperweight. Just behind the seat, against the wall, is a pipe-rack.

'But they won't let me smoke now,' said Jules Verne, in the very accent with which George Meredith once said the same sad thing.

'In this little room are the favourite books, the books one must be able to lay the immediate hand upon.

'You will find all Dickens there,' said Jules Verne, with a glow in his voice. 'As you know, I am a passionate admirer of Dickens. I find he has all things — wit like Sterne, of whom I am a great reader and admirer also; pathos and sentiment of the good alloy, and characters, characters, characters, *à ne pas savoir quoi en faire*. A prodigal, a prodigal, he was like our Balzac, who created a world on which society which came afterwards modelled itself.'

One had come to pity; it was with envy rather that one passed out into the grey and lonely world. For there beyond the velvet hangings stood the table, neatly laid with two covers *vis-à-vis*, by the side of the iris-painted windows, which opened on the sunny gardens full of flowers. And by the sculptured hearth, on the mantelpiece of which a ruddy and resplendent samovar purred its note of intimate and familiar comfort, two armchairs stood side by side.

(*Right*) Kaw-Djer, the 'benefactor' or leader of a small island community of people trying to create an earthly paradise, who finds his plans disrupted when a boat load of emigrants are run ashore, in the novel, *The Jonathan* (1909).

'JULES VERNE AND I'

by H. G. Wells

The balloon accident which pitches a group of people on to a desert island and opens Verne's exciting three-part novel, *The Mysterious Island* (1875).

H. G. Wells, whose early works of science fiction had caused him to be described as 'The English Jules Verne', was by the 1900's also enjoying similar worldwide popularity. Neither author, however, considered himself a rival to the other, and both felt their methods of constructing their stories were different. Wells, in fact, did not reply directly to the challenge Verne made in his interview with Sherard until the 1930's, long after the Frenchman was dead. And what he had to say he confined to a short introduction to a collection of his stories being published in America in 1934. His remarks, though, are an interesting comment by a master of science fiction on his great predecessor.

My tales have been compared with the work of Jules Verne and there was a disposition on the part of literary journalists at one time to call me 'The English Jules Verne'. As a matter of fact there is no literary resemblance whatever between the anticipatory inventions of the great Frenchman and these fantasies. His work dealt almost always with actual possibilities of invention and discovery, and he made some remarkable forecasts.

The interest Verne invoked was a practical one; he wrote and believed and told that this or that thing could be done, which was not at that time done. He helped his reader to imagine it done and to realise what fun, excitement or mischief would ensue. Many of his inventions have 'come true'.

But these stories of mine do not pretend to deal with possible things; they are exercises of the imagination in a quite different field. They belong to a class of writing which includes the *Golden Ass of Apuleius*, *The True Histories of Lucian*, *Peter Schlemil* and the story of *Frankenstein*. It includes, too, some admirable inventions by Mr David Garnett, *Lady into Fox* for instance. They are all fantasies; they do not aim to project a serious possibility;

they aim indeed only at the same amount of conviction as one gets in a good gripping dream. They have to hold the reader to the end by art and illusion and not by proof and argument, and the moment he closes the cover and reflects he wakes up to their impossibility . . .

(*Left*) The new settlers on *The Mysterious Island* train an ape to be their servant. An illustration from the first edition of the book.

(*Below, left*) Captain Nemo is dying and urges the new settlers to leave the island because it is about to be hit by catastrophe: an illustration from the picture strip version of *The Mysterious Island* published by Pendulum Press (1974).

(*Above*) The secret of the island – the submarine *Nautilus* which has been hidden there by Captain Nemo of 'Twenty Thousand Leagues' fame.

(*Below*) The end of *The Mysterious Island* when a volcano erupts: from the Marvel Comics version of the story.

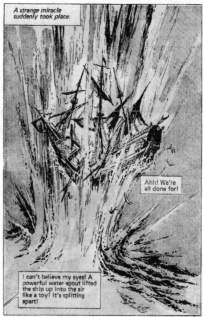

M.G.M.'s silent film version of *The Mysterious Island* made in 1929 introduced several elements not in the Verne story, including strange little creatures rather resembling Donald Duck and a sinister mastermind played by the great Lionel Barrymore.

(*Above*) The more recent version of *The Mysterious Island* starring Herbert Lom stuck much closer to the original (1961).

JULES VERNE AND THE FAIRIES

by Nozière

Jules Verne died on the morning of Friday, March 24, 1905, aged 87 and already a legend in his own lifetime. His novels had carried his genius around the earth and the more famous stories had already been translated into dozens of languages. Yet, as we shall see, his fame was only just beginning. The funeral took place in Amiens on March 28 and was attended by thousands of people of all ages, including many important French dignitaries. An incident which occurred during the ceremony and which has never been properly explained, is now part of literary lore. Among the mourners was a strange, immaculately dressed Englishman who silently approached each member of Verne's family, shook their hands, and solemnly declared (in French): 'Be brave, be brave, in your heavy hour of trial.' As soon as he had passed along the line, the mysterious figure disappeared into the crowds. Was it, some of the family were later to ask themselves, the ghost of Verne's greatest creation, Phileas Fogg? After the funeral, subscriptions were opened to erect a monument to Verne, and apart from the collection and special theatrical performances over the next two years, a columnist in the local paper, *Journal d'Amiens* made a most unconventional appeal in the form of an article, 'Jules Verne and the Fairies' which appeared in the issue of October 15, 1906. The man, Nozière, described an argument among the fairies about the suitability of a monument being erected to a man who some maintained had turned children's minds from magic to science. The appearance here of this unique item, which is now of considerable rarity, marks both its first translation into English and its appearance in book form.

The Children of Captain Grant or *A Voyage Round The World* (1868) as it is sometimes known, is the story of Lord Glenarvan's search for the shipwrecked Captain Grant, which takes him from Britain to South America, and on to Australia and New Zealand.

Walt Disney's *In Search of the Castaways* starring Hayley Mills was based on *The Children of Captain Grant* and contained a memorable performance by Maurice Chevalier.

An illustration from the first English edition of *The Children of Captain Grant* with the youngsters close to finding their father in New Zealand.

The fairies are not dead. They're simply hiding themselves because they fear the glances of the common herd. But at night-fall they still assemble in the woodland, and the autumn evenings are most favourable to their gatherings. Above the streams and over the hills veils are floating: do not mistake them for mists, for they are the diaphanous garments of the fairies, as they come and go. They shake the trees tinted with the gold of autumn; the air is still, and yet a leaf falls: it is some aerial creature which has broken its delicate stem.

They are invisible when the moon hides herself behind the clouds or fails to display herself in the sky. But they appear in the blue radiance, and he who looks for them carefully can see their many-coloured throng. They love the melancholy of the royal parks; they like to be near the springs whose waters no longer flow in the forsaken walks where the pedestals are devoid of their statues. They are as sorrowful as the past and as powers that have fallen.

They have come in large numbers this evening. Here are the enchantresses who challenged the courage and faith of the most Christian knights; here are the godmothers who have watched like true mothers over the fate of the princesses. Here are the evil witches who excel in compounding over

the tombs the philtres of love and of death. They are all talking and gesticulating; but their voices are so soft and their gestures so slight that the silence is hardly broken. Suddenly all are silent and still, for drawn in her mother-of-pearl coach by a hundred dragon-flies with rustling wings, their Queen has just arrived. On the grass the glow-worms gleam and the Queen graciously acknowledges the bows of her sisters.

'Sisters,' she says, 'why have you called us together? Why have you aroused me from my divine meditation? Are you considering the mad idea of once more reigning over

mankind? Are you thinking of enchanting the fierce warriors, as in the time of the crusaders you kept them from destroying the precious mosques and the masterpieces of eastern art? What event has been serious enough to make you leave your rest?'

The fairy Carabosse rises and replies:

'Queen, because my face is ugly, I'm said to cherish the evil powers of envy. But I'm proud of my power. Envy inspires courage and skill: envy shows the giants to be only dwarfs on tip-toe; envy keeps men from an excess of admiration, from the dangers of worshipping their fellows. So my sisters have asked me to speak for them all, and so I dare to tell you what they wish.

'Although you are our queen, rulers sometimes do not know what their subjects know; you, no doubt, have heard it rumoured that the French want to raise statues to Jules Verne. In a few days the Chatelet Theatre will give a special performance, and the proceeds will go to swell the coffers meant to pay for the sculptors and the marble. Shall we endure such a scandal? Shall we allow monuments to be erected to the enemy of our race? What! His image to be raised in Nantes where he was born, in Amiens where he worked, even in Paris! If we have any power at all, we will not let such a proposal be carried out.

'Has your Majesty forgotten the harm Jules Verne has done us? Admittedly before he wrote his wretched stories, men and women alike have forsaken our altars, but the children were still faithful to us. They hoped that on some fine day they would meet us at some turning on the path, and that our word would give them strength and wealth. They respected us.

'Jules Verne has given them a new ideal. He has unscrupulously turned their young minds away from us. He has embued the children with a dislike for the supernatural; he has incited them to despair fairy stories and to sound the depths of science. We used to utter magic words whose power the children could admire. For their strange sounds Jules Verne has substituted algebraical formulae and equations: he has rashly extolled the power of reason.

'He was our supreme enemy and in fighting us he sought to suppress the last traces of the old religion. What are we, if not the heirs of the ancient gods? To explain thunder, the ancestors invented Jupiter, and they imagined Neptune to account for the movements of the waves. We did not come into the world, like the Olympians to explain the unknown causes of physical facts: our mission

was higher, because we symbolise the capriciousness of nature.

'People wondered why this man was intelligent and that man dull; why this girl was beautiful and that girl ugly: they were inclined to be wrathful against such wrongs. But they accepted them when they learned that it was our whims which distributed virtue or vice, wealth or poverty, to the newly-born. Frail mortals were satisfied when they realised the apparent causes of the injustices which beset them and they were resigned to their sufferings when they fancied they understood that these are inevitable. It was for this reason that religion had so long and so profound an effect upon them.

'But without revolting against the established forms of worship, without openly declaring war upon us, Jules Verne has persuaded the children that they must not rely upon chance, which means our help, to be happy. He has stimulated their energy. He has extolled the beauty of work and the wealth of the human mind. All who wake the pride of these wretched mortals are our enemies. As soon as an author advises his fellows to think and to act, it is clear that he is committing an offence against divinity. Of yore, those who preached such doctrines would be burned. Today, statues are raised to them.

'The mighty beings who are adored in the temples refrain from punishing those who deny them; but we have decided to act against the one who had completed the work of destroying our prestige. We shall murmur into the ears of men the lying words they are always ready to hear; we shall tell them that Jules Verne does not deserve their admiration and that it would be absurd to raise statues to him. They will gladly welcome our words, for they are always pleased to have a pretext for not honouring one of their fellows and for not spending a little cash.'

The fairies showed by their applause how completely they approved of these words. But then the Queen spoke.

'I can see,' she began 'that you are strangely lacking in political sense. Why should we be so anxious to proclaim that a mighty being is our enemy? We should first try to show that, even if appearances are against him, he is our friend. This is a watchword of excellent value on which you could not meditate too long.

'Do not say that Jules Verne was our enemy. No doubt he honoured reason and science. But he was a very skilful magician. I can see in your midst Cinderella's fairy godmother, who transformed a pumpkin into a coach to take her to the royal ball. Can that be compared with the wonderful *Nautilus*

The Adventures of Captain Hatteras (1866) gives a remarkable picture of life on board a ship exploring the Arctic: all the more remarkable when it is remembered that Verne had never been there. The illustrations here are from two turn-of-the-century editions of the first volume of the book entitled, *The English at the North Pole*.

(*Facing page*) A picture from the French edition of the second volume of Captain Hatteras's adventures, *Le Désert de Glace, The Field of Ice*.

which took Captain Nemo into the depths of the sea, which enabled him to recover the wealth swallowed up by the waves, and to gather from the gulf the most rare of pearls? The wolf who swallowed Red Riding Hood is no more terrible than the condor which carried off the son of Captain Grant. The fairy Carabosse has just evoked the mythologies. But does it not recall the wanderings of Ulysses when you hear of the adventures of Phileas Fogg, who went round the world in eighty days?

'Jules Verne has shown us men who struggle against the whims of the elements and against the wickedness of men. Robur who sought to conquer the air and to steer his aircraft is a brother of the rash Icarus. The mysterious Captain Nemo who descends into the depths of the waters, was he not led on by the song of the sirens? When Captain Hatteras rushes blindly up the snow-clad heights, does it not recall the giants who sought to attack the sky?

'Jules Verne has been faithful to all our fables because mankind has always had to face the same problems. For thousands of years mortal men have sought to control the forces of the universe. They have adored the statues of the gods, they have asked the help of our magic wands. What help have they had from the Olympians and from ourselves? Sure of our protection, they have had more confidence in their own energy and their reasoning powers. For centuries they have begged supernatural forces to sustain and direct them. So they have gained a divine spark; it is the fire which Prometheus stole from the mortals and whose flames we have fanned.

'Do not let us grow angry with that flame; it is we who have fanned it. Let us take care not to hate Jules Verne, for he is our godson and he has loved us tenderly. In his works you will find spirits good and evil. Ayrton, who directs a vessel along a false course, is he not a spirit of evil? And the savant Paganel, does he not seem like a guardian angel?* Jules Verne adored the fairies. If you doubt this, think of the fierce hero who in *The Begum's Fortune*, constructed a terrible gun to destroy a whole city. The gun is fired, but the terrible shell misses its mark, it passes overhead, it loses itself in the sky and becomes a star. You can see that Jules Verne was a poet and that we can never hate him.

'Nor must we forget, my sisters, that our hate would be powerless. We must

* Ayrton and Paganel are characters in Jules Verne's story *The Children of Captain Grant.*

give way to facts. Men admire that author who has foretold such great discoveries, and they piously cherish his memory because he charmed their youth and because he still delights their children. Think of all the little ones who excitedly open the volumes with their gilt edges and with their covers decorated with ships and balloons and stars! Where have not their glowing imaginations been led? After Cyrano de Bergerac and before Wells, he took them to the moon: who knows whether, within a few years, that journey will not be possible? Have not the submarines fulilled the forecast of the *Nautilus*? He was a prophet in his own country.

'When his statue is erected, all that we shall ask is that we may appear around its base. For we must not fail to remember that we have not been foreign to the development of his imagination. We made him other gifts; from us he received a real power of working, great modesty, great goodness. He lived a retired life, far from honours, and he has accomplished a colossal task. He has fallen asleep bravely like a good workman whose labour is done. Do not let us be afraid to pay homage to him who took our place and who has shown himself able to carry on our wonderful work.'

We do not know whether her subjects accepted the opinion of their Queen. Just as they were about to take a vote, the moon appeared and the fairies vanished into the night.

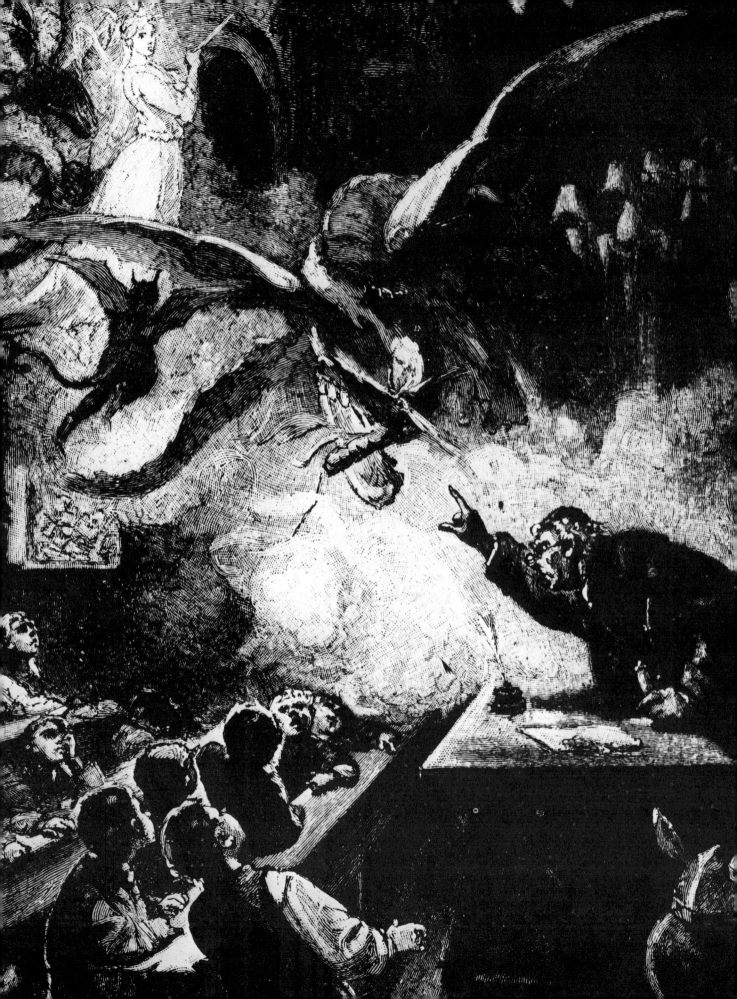

The Castle of the Carpathians which Verne published in 1892 is one of his least known and most undervalued titles. According to critic Gavin Ewart it 'may have been one of Bram Stoker's source books for *Dracula*' and certainly its employment of ghosts, vampires and other elements of the supernatural make it unique among the *Voyages Extraordinaires*. Set in Gothic countryside, it recounts how the eccentric Baron Gortz recreates in his castle the beautiful opera singer he admired from afar until her sudden death in mid-performance. That the seemingly life-like creature is finally revealed as a reflection and her voice a recording does not detract from the excitement and tension of the story.

Jules Verne, the Master Storyteller of Exploits on Land, Sea and Air. These illustrations are for *Adventures of Three Russians and Three Englishmen in South Africa* (1872), *Journey to the Centre of the Earth* (1864) and *The Master of the World* (1904).

HOMAGE TO JULES VERNE

by Michel Butor

It is perhaps not surprising that the achievements in space flight by the Russians and Americans in the late 1950s and 60s, plus the growing importance of Science Fiction as a genre, should have brought about a revival of interest in Jules Verne. While it is certainly true that for the first half of this century, Verne was mainly thought of as a 'children's author' and only his acknowledged masterpieces were kept in print, there was no denying a growing realisation in literary and scientific circles that much that he had predicted *was* coming true. Appropriately enough it was in France that the revival got under way with several exhibitions about his work and the reprinting of many of his *Voyages Extraordinaires*. In England, the life-long Verne enthusiast I. O. Evans dedicated himself to the task of singlehandedly preparing new translations of all the 65 titles in the series, while in America several journalists, led by Michael Slonim of the *New York Times* began to devote columns to Verne's prophecy. (The film companies, too, have not been slow to see the potential in several of Verne's stories, though in most cases it has to be said that as is so often the case, the end product bears little relation to the originals!) Here, then, is an article by the French journalist and literary critic, Michel Butor, spotlighting this development: the translation is from *The New Statesman* of July 15, 1966.

JULES VERNE

We've recently been fêting Jules Verne in France, with new editions, exhibitions and the like. It is gradually becoming apparent that this 'children's' author is not only one of our most popular writers but also one of the most extraordinary.

At one time, there were no children's books. Fairy-tales? These were only collected into books with Perrault in France and the brothers Grimm in Germany. Children's books were school books, books in the languages taught in schools: that's to say, Greek and Latin literature. Parents read novels, periodicals and lampoons; their children read Homer, Virgil and Plutarch. The province of childhood was antiquity. When adult literature finally abandoned Latin, leaving it to embark, for a second time, on its long last gasp, a children's literature in the popular tongue was needed to bridge the gap between their parents' classical childhood and their own. The case was met by a trip into antiquity.

Reread *The Adventures of Telemachus*, or *Young Anacharsis's Travels in Greece* by the Abbé Barthélemy.

From the 18th century, if not before, French society considered that its literature was not 'good for children'. It had to be censored. But it wasn't only that it said too much: it said too little, too. Basic aspects of reality were inadequately treated. This deficiency was hardly remedied by the lives of the saints (the Bible was only read in Protestant families) and selected pieces from classical literature (children were no longer taught to 'dive in' as they once had been). And so we find a corpus of children's literature growing up, books which every well-brought-up child read outside school and which constituted a kind of extramural education.

Perrault's fairy-tales form part of this, of course, but so do three works not written for children at all, works so difficult to read that to this day abridged or expurgated editions and feeble imitations abound: *The Arabian Nights*, *Gulliver's Travels* and *Robinson Crusoe*.

Different as they are, these three works have one thing in common: they are 'extraordinary voyages', just as *Telemachus* and *Anacharsis* were. For the child, imprisoned in the adult world, they open a window on the outer world and on the past. Some of the heroes are children (Aladdin, Man Friday, Gulliver in Brobdingnag), but this prime ingredient of fairy-tales, which set out to preach conduct to the young reader, as did the Countess de Ségur, is here attributable to the fact that when a grown-up lands on an unknown shore he becomes a child again.

The child finds himself on the outside of that adult fortress which is unbreachable save by exams and ceremonies, whose walls cut off the rest of the world. Just as the schoolchild of the past, from the heights of 'antiquity', was a severe judge of the 'leaden century' into which the great people of the past had fallen, so the schoolchild of recent times, *'amoureux de cartes et d'estampes'*, returns from his imaginary travels to the discovery that his parents' world is a mere province. Note the part played by Russia in the stories of the Countess de Ségur.

Family Without A Name (1889) Verne's Canadian novel dealing with the vexed problem of Quebec, which the book shows he had thoroughly researched. The dramatic adventures of the hero, Jean, in his fight for freedom, have caused the work to be compared to that of the great Fennimore Cooper.

FAMILLE SANS NOM

JULES VERNE

G. TIRET-BOGNET

When he gave up putting on shows for adults and decided to write 'for children', for the *Magasin d'Education et de Récréation*, Jules Verne chose to explore the rest of the world. With encyclopedic diligence he gathered together the entire literature of travels – describing worlds known only to certain adults or allowing us to imagine unknown worlds where no one has ever set foot but whose existence is nonetheless undeniable – in order to create for children a world outside that of their parents, a world unknown to their parents. The fact that this new image of the world is methodically constructed from what adults cannot challenge or deny helps to sustain the image once the child has grown to manhood. The works of Jules Verne, in all their modesty, play a decisive role in relation to that world civilisation which is now painfully emerging.

The villainous Kongra the Wrecker who pounces on helpless vessels off Tierra del Fuego until the building of *The Lighthouse at the End of the World* (1905).

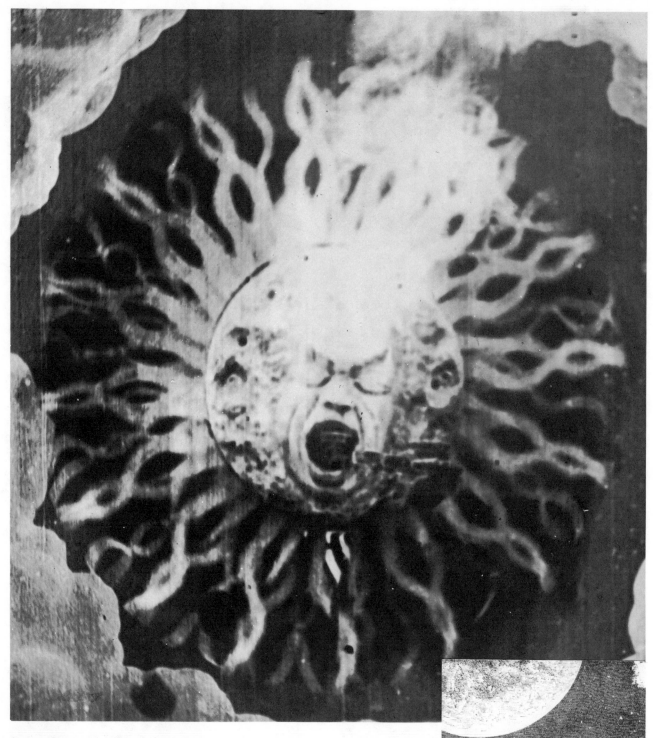

Georges Méliès' film *An Impossible Voyage* (1904) drew on Verne's *From the Earth to the Moon* for inspiration, but the movie's 'flying train' went all the way to the sun and back!

An engraving from the original edition of *From the Earth to the Moon*, showing *The Columbiad* space-craft approaching the moon (1865).

ASTRONAUT BY GASLIGHT

by William Golding

Over recent years a number of distinguished writers have attempted to explain Verne's talent and the importance of his work. Each new edition of one or more of his books has brought forth fresh reviews — and still more opinions. In my view the most interesting, objective, and yet by no means idolatrous, consideration of his achievement is the review which follows by William Golding, from *The Spectator* of June 9, 1961. Mr Golding, I perhaps need hardly remind you, is the author of that modern classic, *The Lord of the Flies* (1954) and in several of his other works has shown himself a master of fantasy fiction.

A child's ignorant eye can make a Western out of a Dumas tapestry. Many of us can remember the quality of the Western:

> I will reward you, my dear, by passing that time with you, which I intended to pass with your mistress.

The years have taught us that D'Artagnan did not pass the time in showing Kitty those tricks of fence with which he and/or Douglas Fairbanks was able to pink a brace of opponents. As for La Vallière, Buckingham and the Queen, as for the ladders and trapdoors, the assignations and *billets-doux*, the hissing, tittering complications — I, personally, am stunned when I think what a passionless pattern I made of it all. If we revisit our childhood's reading, we are likely to discover that we missed the satire of *Gulliver*, the evangelism of *Pilgrim's Progress* and the loneliness of *Robinson Crusoe*.

But when we revisit some books in this way, we find that the iridescent film has burst, to leave nothing behind but a wet mark. Henty, Ballantyne, Burroughs, require an innocence of approach which, while it is natural enough to a child, would be a mark of puerility in an adult. I declare this with

some feeling, since during the last week or so I have undertaken a long course of Jules Verne; and suffer at the moment, not from indigestion so much as hunger.

Yet once these books* satisfied me. They held me rapt. I dived with the *Nautilus*, was shot round the moon, crossed Darkest Africa in a balloon, descended to the centre of the earth, drifted in the South Atlantic, dying of thirst, and tasted — oh rapture! It always sent me indoors for a drink —

Journey to the Centre of the Earth, 20,000 Leagues Under the Sea, From the Earth to the Moon, Round the Moon, Five Weeks in a Balloon, At the North Pole, The Wilderness of Ice and Propellor Island. (Arco, 1961.)

the fresh waters of the Amazon. And now?

Of course the books have not vanished wholly. They have the saving grace of gusto. Verne had his generation's appetite for facts, and he serves them up in *grande cuisine*: 'How amazing . . . were the microscopical jellyfish observed by Scoresby in the Greenland seas, which he estimated at 23,898,000,000,000,000,000 in an area of two square miles!' But a diet of such creatures palls, for Verne's verbal

Propellor Island (1895) Verne's ingenious novel of a floating land-mass which can be driven anywhere at sea thus enabling its wealthy inhabitants to live in perpetual summer conditions. This illustration was by Hayes for the Panther paperback edition in 1965.

A remarkable still from Méliès' *An Impossible Voyage* showing the band of explorers in their machine which can travel beneath the ocean as well as in the heavens. The party is lead by Engineer Crazyloff and includes Professor Polehunter, Secretary Rattlebrains, and Officers Easy-fooled, Daredevil and Schemer!

(*Opposite*) The most famous of Méliès' films, *A Trip to the Moon*, which parodied Verne's moon voyage, appeared in 1902. Méliès was producer, director, scriptwriter, set designer, costumier and lead actor of the film, although he did employ some of the delightful girls from the Folies-Bergère to play the moon people called Selenites! Romance reared its head in the modern version of *From the Earth to the Moon* starring Debra Paget and George Sanders (1958).

surface lacks the slickness of the professional; it is turgid and slack by turns. Only the brio of his enthusiasm carries us forward from one adventure to another. What is left for the adult is off-beat; something so specialised that to enjoy it is about as eccentric as collecting the vocal chords of prima donnas. For Verne attracts today, not so much by his adventures as by the charm of his nineteenth-century interiors. The lamplight lies cosily on thick curtains and elaborate tables. Clubs are as rich and secure as an Egyptian tomb. They have no servant problem, the carpets are never worn, and the subscription will never go up. Here live the savants, and a savant is related to a scientist as an antiquary is to an archæologist. He is a learned enthusiast, a man of boundless absurdity, energy and stubbornness. At any moment he may leap from his hip-bath, sell his Consols and buy 1,866 gallons of sulphuric acid, 16,050 pounds of iron and 11,600 square feet of twilled Lyons silk coated with gutta-percha. His oath is 'A thousand

thunders!' Cross him, and he will dash his smoking-cap into the grate. Take leave to doubt his wisdom and he will attempt to assault you. Held back by force, he will wager a fortune on the outcome of his adventure. Without knowing it, he passes a large part of his life under the influence of alcohol, for at the touch of success he will dash off, or drain off, or toss off, a bumper of brandy, which he follows with an endless succession of toasts. This half-

gallon or so of brandy has as little effect on him as whisky has on the tough hero of a television serial. Indeed, his euphoria has always been indistinguishable from intoxication. Champollion is his ancestor in the real world, and Conan Doyle's professor in *The Lost World* his literary descendant.

This typification is moderated but not destroyed by national distinction. Verne reserved, as was perhaps natural, his greatest *élan* for the

French, or at least, the Europeans. He divided sang-froid between the English and the American. All these qualities, and others, are laid on with the trowel of farce. Indeed, the sang-froid of his Englishman, Mr. Phileas Fogg, is at times indistinguishable from advanced schizophrenia. But when his characters let themselves go – here is Captain Nemo expressing his sense of displeasure:

Captain Nemo was before me but I could hardly recognise him. His face was transfigured. His eyes flashed sullenly; his teeth were set; his taut body, clenched fists, and head hunched between his shoulders, betrayed the violent agitation that pervaded his whole frame. He did not move. My telescope, fallen from his hands, had rolled at his feet.

I must remember that these jerky cut-outs once convinced me, moved me, excited me, as they still move children. They fit our picture of the nineteenth century. What about the Marquis of Anglesey and the Duke of Wellington at Waterloo?
'By G—d Sir, I have lost my leg.'
'By G—d Sir, so you have.' If that had not been a real exchange, Verne would have invented it.
What the child misses most in these books – if I am anything to go by – is the fact that Verne was a heavy-handed satirist. The organisation which fires its shot at the moon is the Gun Club of Boston. These were the savants who engaged in the arms race of the American Civil War.

Their military weapons attained colossal proportions, and their projectiles, exceeding the prescribed limits, unfortunately occasionally cut in two some unoffending bystanders. These inventions, in fact, left far in the rear the timid instruments of European artillery.

After that we are not surprised to learn that the honour accorded to the members of the Gun Club was 'proportional to the masses of their guns, and in the direct ratio of the square of the distances attained by their projectiles.' Their personal appearance is at once ludicrous and horrifying:

(*Facing page*) The remarkable 'electrics' used by the mysterious scientist Dr Antekirtt to defend his island off the coast of Tripoli in the novel, *Mathias Sandorf* (1885).

The Aerial Village (1901) the story of a German savant in the African jungle trying to learn the language of animals who also stumbles across a half-human 'lost race'.

Crutches, wooden legs, artificial arms, steel hooks, caoutchouc jaws, silver craniums, platinum noses, were all to be found; and it was calculated by the great statistician Pitcairn that throughout the Gun Club there was not quite one arm between four persons, and exactly two legs between six. Nevertheless, these valiant artillerists took no particular account of these little facts, and felt justly proud when the dispatches of a battle returned the number of victims at tenfold the quantity of the projectiles expended.

Throughout the seventeen books there is an almost total absence of women. Verne was honester here than some of his SF descendants who lug in a blonde for the look of the thing.

His male world was probably all he could manage. You cannot hack out a woman's face with an axe; he could not, or would not, write about women. He remains the only French writer who could get his hero right round the world without meeting more than one woman while he was doing it.

Verne's talent was not spurred by a love of what we should not call pure science, but by technology. His books are the imaginative counterpart of the Great Eastern, the Tay Bridge, or the Great Steam Flying Machine. It is this which accounts for his continued appeal to subadolescent boyhood. For the science sides of our schools are crammed to bursting with boys who have confused a genial enjoyment in watching wheels go round with the

pursuit of knowledge. His heroes, too, are a pattern of what the twelve-year-old boy considers a proper adult pattern — they are tough, sexless, casually brave, resourceful, and *making something big*. Compared with the Sheriff of Dumb Valley, or the Private Eye, they constitute no mean ideal; to the adult, their appeal is wholly nostalgic. Apart from the odd touch that convinces — the pleasures of Professor Aronnax when, after years of groping for fish, he observes them through the windows of the Nautilus; the willingness of the Frenchman to go to the moon with no prospect of coming back — apart from this they are a dead loss.

A study of Verne makes me uncomfortable. It seems that on the level of engineering, predictions can be made that will come true. So the soberer SF is no more than a blueprint for tomorrow. In time we can expect to see photographs — TV programmes — of acrobats performing on the moon, beneath the blue domes of Lunarville. The hot-spot which lies near the gantries of Marsport, that sleazy cantonment peopled with whisky-slinging space pilots and interplanetary whores, is a fact of the twenty-first century. This prospect would not dismay me, had one of Verne's characters not suggested that the heating of a colossal boiler to three million degrees would one day destroy the world; and I find the third suggestion nearer than the others.

Nevertheless, Verne's nineteenth-century technology and mania for size sometimes result in a combination which has a charm to be found nowhere else. He was excited with arc lighting and gives us a picture with all the fascination of an early lantern slide. Light itself, sheer brilliance, is an enchantment to him, when it is produced by man. In *The Wilderness of Ice*, we can share a forgotten moment. Today, the light of an atomic explosion is a savage thing which blinds and burns. We have gone as far as our eyes can go. If we want to discover a new quality in light, we have to return to the pit lamp, or candle. But to Verne, the white-hot carbon was a near-miracle:

Then two pieces of carbon rod, placed in the lantern at the proper distance, were gradually brought closer together, and an intense light, which the wind could not dim nor diminish, sprang from the lantern. It was marvellous to see these rays, whose glory rivalled the whiteness of the [snowy] plain, and which made all the projections round it visible by their shadow.

Perhaps the best moment comes when we get a mixture of the fantastic, but future and possible, with the ordinary paraphernalia of nineteenth-century living. In *Round the Moon*, the three voyagers move about their spaceship, peering delightedly at this and that. In the shadow of the earth all is dark; but as they move into the sun's rays, they find them shining *up* through the base of the ship — and are able to turn off the light, in order to save gas.

Lastly I must mention a splendid picture from the original edition of this book, which the publishers, to their great credit, have preserved for posterity. It is a, or rather *the*, moment of free fall — not the modern sort which can be endless, but the nineteenth-century sort, the point where earth and moon gravity is equal. The three voyagers, dressed as for a stroll in the park *circa* 1860, are helpless in the air, as are the dog and the two hens. A telescope and top hat hang near them. The walls of the spaceship are padded, but the padding has the effect of ornate wallpaper. The three gentlemen, a little startled, but not distressingly so, hang over their shadows. Softly, the gaslight pours down.

(*Below*) One of the less distinguished film versions of Verne's work, *Rocket to the Moon* (1967) with Troy Donahue and Lionel Jeffries.

(*Facing page*) The bizarre picture of the astronauts' dog, Satellite, floating alongside the space shell as it orbits the planet in *Round The Moon* (1870).

'A GREAT PIONEER OF THE SPACE AGE'

Verne, of course, did not live to see more than a few of his prophecies come true, but his descendants and the dedicated members of the *Société Jules Verne* in Paris — which has now been in existence for over half a century — have observed with ever increasing delight as his fiction has become fact. It fell to Verne's grandson, Jean-Jules Verne, the third (and only surviving) child of Michael Verne, the author's sole heir, to see the greatest triumph of the master's predictions when men reached the Moon in 1969. M. Jean-Jules, a life-long member of the French judiciary, was twelve when his grandfather died, but retained vivid memories of him and his work which he utilised in a fascinating biography, *Jules Verne* published in 1973. The following newspaper report describes M. Verne's involvement with the moon landing . . .

On the evening of July 20, 1969 when man finally achieved his dream of standing on the Moon, one person experienced particuar feelings of satisfaction mingled with natural delight at the achievement. He is M. Jean-Jules Verne, a relative of the man who first realistically projected the idea of space flight to the Moon.

M. Verne, the grandson of the founder of Science Fiction, Jules Verne, is now a retired chairman of the Toulon Bench, but naturally takes a very keen interest in all the developments of the space age. Immediately after the successful landing on the Moon, he told journalists, 'I have been invited to Cape Kennedy to be present at the triumph of my grandfather's ideas. Do you recall that phrase, "Whatever a man is capable of imagining, another is capable of achieving"? Well, as has just been proved, the poets are always right!'

Later, when the Apollo 11 had returned safely to Earth, M. Verne revealed what he considered an even more dramatic realisation of his grandfather's prophecy.

'Verne's eminently *scientific* fiction actually never received a finer consecration than the earlier mission of Apollo 8 which took place a hundred years after his book, *De la Terre à la Lune*, appeared,' he said, disclosing that he had received a letter from Frank Borman, one of the members of the crew of the spacecraft.

' "It cannot be a mere matter of coincidence," Frank Borman wrote to me, "Our space vehicle was launched from Florida, like Barbicane's; it had the same weight and the same height, and it splashed down in the Pacific a mere two and a half miles from the point mentioned in the novel." Borman told me as well — which is proof enough of the power of Verne's fiction as such — that his wife, having read Part One of the Moon story, was terrified that he might never come back. He suggested she read Part Two!'

'I must also mention the final accolade this brave astronaut paid my grandfather, for they are words which I heartily endorse myself, "In a very real sense Jules Verne is one of the great pioneers of the space age." '

La Monde November, 1969.

(*Opposite*) A remarkably prophetic cover of *Amazing Stories* for February 1928. The similarity between this 'New Earth' and the 'Death Star' in George Lucas's film *Star Wars* is quite uncanny! The issue featured Verne's *The Master of the World.*

Verne's fiction becomes fact — the American astronaut Edwin 'Buzz' Aldrin on the surface of the moon after the landing of Apollo II in July 1969.

'MY SPIRIT·TELEPHONE CONVERSATION WITH JULES VERNE'

by Erich Von Däniken

The books of the now world-famous Swiss author, Erich von Däniken, including *Chariots of the Gods* (1968) and *The Gold of the Gods* (1972) in which he sets out to try and prove that in prehistoric and early historic times the Earth was visited by beings from space, have been greeted in many quarters with the same kind of amazement and sceptism which greeted Jules Verne's first science fiction stories. Without wishing to take any side in the controversy, there is no denying the intriguing nature of von Däniken's theories nor the enormous popularity of his books. On more than one occasion, he has expressed himself a fan of Verne's work and in his latest book, *According to the Evidence* (1977) actually claims to have made contact with the spirit of the departed author to discuss his latest ideas. The extract is reprinted here to demonstrate how 'alive' Verne's memory continues to be . . .

An hour ago a leading medium succeeded in putting me in telephonic communication with Jules Verne, the forerunner of the science fiction novelist, who died in 1905. I was anxious to ask the old gentleman for advice, because I was afraid my imagination might run away with me.

I reproduce the spirit-telephone conversation literally:

'Von Däniken here. Honoured master, I have just come back from America.'

'How do you do, Mr von Däniken. You did it in five and a half hours, I know. My crazy idea of a journey round the world in eighty days has long been obsolete. I would give a lot to live in your day.'

'All the same you were ahead of your time once. But that's not what I want to talk to you about.'

'If you are making forecasts about the future, I can give you one good piece of advice. From now on proceed from realistic assumptions.'

'It was precisely about that point I wanted to ask your opinion. I am proposing to claim in my new book that by around the year 2000 there could be a city in space with 10,000 inhabitants living, working, researching, producing, raising children and

The 'neutral helicoidal ray' devised by scientist Zephirin Xirdal in *The Chase of the Golden Meteor* (1908) to bring down to earth a solid gold meteorite discovered in the heavens. However, the frenzy of greed among the public which awaits the landing of the meteor causes Xirdal to modify his plans and at the last moment change its course so that it falls into the sea.

feeding themselves, and that they will even supply people on earth with energy. What do you think of that idea? Is it unreasonable?'

(I got no answer. There was a rushing noise in the air. When it died down, I asked again.)

'Do you think I ought to put this idea before my readers?'

'Excuse me, Mr. von Däniken, I had to laugh and some of the eminent men floating about near me are bursting their sides with laughter, too. Perhaps you heard them? How do you get such absurd ideas? I must warn you against writing anything like that. No one will publish a word of it. A space station with 10,000 people! No, keep your imagination on the ground and stick to what is technically feasible.

All right. Following the advice of the ancestor of science fiction, I *am* sticking to what is technically feasible. In front of me I have four newspaper sources which have this to say about the technical possibilities of the project: 'The idea of a space station for 10,000 people is within the bounds of technology and is already technically possible. A group of 28 professors and technicians who were commissioned by Stanford University and NASA to

The Testament of an Eccentric (1899) describes the bizarre will of an American millionaire who bequeaths his fortune to whichever of the possible heirs can most quickly reach a number of points chosen at random in the United States. The surprise ending to the novel owes much to Poe's influence on Verne – for the eccentric suddenly rises from his coffin to announce that he has been in a cataleptic trance!

examine the problem came to this conclusion. The space station, which would be about equidistant (384,000 km) from the earth and the moon and would cost about 100 milliard dollars could be finished by the end of the century. It would be built in a two-stage programme. First an earth orbiting 2,000 man space station and a smaller moon station would have to be constructed. From there all the building materials, made from lunar mat-erials, would be transported and assembled in space. Only carbon, hydrogen and nitrogen would have to be supplied from earth. The finished space station, which would revolve once a minute to produce artificial gravity, would have all the vital necessities on board: fields and meadows would stretch for 800 m before the eyes of its inhabitants, the drinking water would be constantly regenerated, the air would be cleaner than it is over our terrestrial cities . . .'

During my next telephone call to the aged Jules Verne, I shall tell him that I have kept my feet on the ground of what is technically possible. He won't laugh this time!

Detectives investigating a murder in *Les Frères Kip* (1902) find the images of the guilty man imprinted on a photograph of the pupils of the victim's eyes. This idea was based on an old superstition which is said to have some basis in fact, and clearly fascinated Verne.

En l'année 1872, la maison portant le numéro 7 de Saville-row, Burlington Gardens — maison dans laquelle Sheridan mourut en 1814 — était habitée par Philéas Fogg, esq., l'un des membres les plus singuliers et les plus remarqués du Reform-Club de Londres, bien qu'il semblât prendre à tâche de ne rien faire qui pût attirer l'attention.

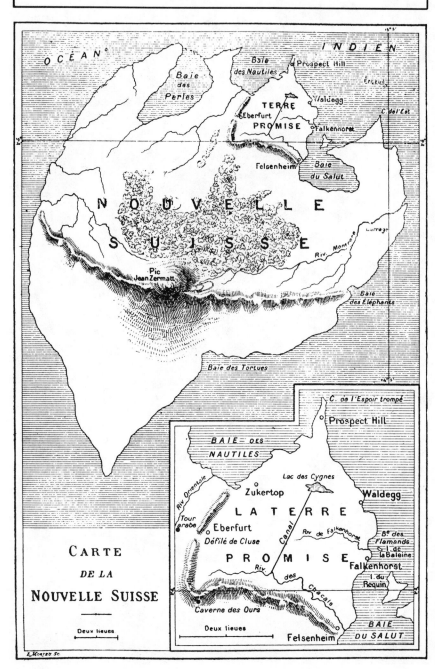

CARTE
DE LA
NOUVELLE SUISSE

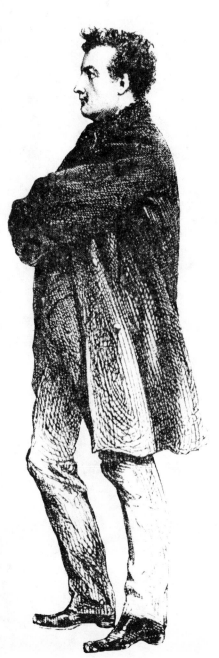

Verne loved the sea, and it was on his yacht, the *St. Michel* that he wrote much of *Twenty Thousand Leagues Under The Sea* between 1867 and 1870. Also shown here are illustrations from two more of his sea stories *L'Invasion De La Mer* (1905) in which an earthquake aids in the building of a canal, and *Dick Sands, Boy Captain* (1878) about an intrepid young seaman who proves himself the master of hurricanes at sea and the determined champion of the oppressed on land.

LA JOURNÉE D'UN JOURNALISTE AMÉRICAIN EN 2889

by Jules Verne

This final item is perhaps the most unusual of all Jules Verne's tales of prophecy — and as much of what it forecasts is still far in the future, it is a most suitable item with which to close this book. As I mentioned in my introduction, the story was written for an American newspaper editor, Gordon Bennett, and appeared in the magazine, *The Forum* in 1889. I have already gone into its background there, but I should just like to quote Verne's biographer, Marguerite Allotte de la Fuye on its importance: 'In this story, under the guise of wilful fantasy, he puts forward the most staggering hypotheses on the organisation of the capital cities of the future. He foresees and describes aerial buses and trains, advertisements projected on the clouds, and newspapers giving a picture in vision and sound of world events at the same moment they are taking place. In these great cities of the future, the telegraph has to be replaced by the phono-telephoto. Jules Verne even spoke of selenium as the agent to be used in transmitting visual images: and it was indeed this non-metallic element, with its special conductor qualities, which was to be employed sixteen years later, when the earliest types of television apparatus came to be made. He also foresaw new types of accumulators, which would store up the energy of the sun's rays, the electricity within the earth itself, and the power derived from waterfalls, rivers, winds and tides. Transformers would draw off this vital energy, and after putting it to work, would ultimately restore it to its original sources. The excess of summer heat would also be stored up and released in the winter months, so that winter would cease to exist.' Whether this particular story will add further credit to the prophetic genius of Jules Verne only time will tell!

Edouard Riou's illustration for the American publication of *The Day of an American Journalist in 2889*.

The pictures which accompany this reprint of Verne's short story are taken from the first French edition of *Robur le Conquérant* (1885) published by Hetzel, and the English translation of its sequel *The Master of the World* which appeared in the *Boy's Own Paper* in 1914. W. H. G. Kingston, who was editor of *B.O.P.*, was also a regular translator of Verne's works.

In the Twenty-ninth Century

the Day of an American Journalist in 2889

by Jules Verne

The men of the twenty-ninth century live in a perpetual fairyland, though they do not seem to realise it. Bored with wonders, they are cold towards everything that progress brings them every day. It all seems only natural.

If they compared it with the past, they would better appreciate what our civilisation is, and realise what a road it has traversed. What would then seem finer than our modern cities, with streets a hundred yards wide, with buildings a thousand feet high, always at an equable temperature, and the sky furrowed by thousands of aero-cars and aero-'buses! Compared with these towns, whose population may include up to ten million inhabitants, what were those villages, those hamlets of a thousand years ago, that Paris, that London, that New York — muddy and badly ventilated townships, traversed by jolting contraptions, hauled along by horses — yes! by horses! it's unbelievable!

If they recalled the erratic working of the steamers and the railways, their many collisions, and their slowness, how greatly would travellers value the aero-trains, and especially these pneumatic tubes laid beneath the oceans, which convey them with a speed of a thousand miles an hour? And would they not enjoy the telephone and the telephote even better if they recollected that our fathers were reduced to that antediluvial apparatus which they called the 'telegraph?'

It's very strange. These surprising transformations are based on principles which were quite well known to our ancestors, although these, so to speak, made no use of them. Heat, steam, electricity, are as old as mankind. Towards the end of the nineteenth century, did not the savents declare that the only difference between the physical and chemical forces consists of the special rates of vibration of the etheric particles?

As so enormous a stride had been made, that of recognising the mutual relationship of all these forces, it is incredible that it took so long to work out the rates of vibration that differentiate between them. It is especially surprising that the method of passing directly from one to another, and of producing one without the other, has only been discovered so recently.

So it was however, that things happened, and it was only in 2790, about a hundred years ago, that the famous Oswald Nyer succeeded in doing so.

A real benefactor of humanity, that great man! His achievement, a work of genius, was the parent of all the others! A constellation of inventors was born out of it, culminating in our extraordinary James Jackson. It is to

THE "ALBATROSS"

him that we owe the new accumulators, some of which condense the force of the solar rays, others the electricity stored in the heart of our globe, and yet again others, energy coming from any source whatever, whether it be the waterfalls, winds, or rivers. It is to him that we owe no less the transformer which, at a touch on a simple switch, draws on the force that lives in the accumulators and releases it as heat, light, electricity, or mechanical power after it has performed any task we need.

Yes, it was from the day on which these two appliances were thought out that progress really dates. They have given mankind almost an infinite power. Through mitigating the bleakness of winter by restoring to it the excessive heat of the summer, they have revolutionised agriculture. By providing motive power for the appliances used in aerial navigation, they have enabled commerce to make a splendid leap forward. It is to them that we owe the unceasing production of electricity without either batteries or machines, light without combustion or incandescence, and finally that inexhaustible source of energy which has increased industrial production a hundred-fold.

Very well then! The whole of these wonders, we shall meet them in an incomparable office-block — the office of the *Earth Herald*, recently inaugurated in the 16823rd Avenue.

If the founder of the *New York Herald*, Gordon Bennett, were to be born a second time today, what would he say when he saw this palace of marble and gold that belongs to his illustrious descendant, Francis Bennett? Thirty generations had followed one another, and the *New York Herald* had always stayed in that same Bennett family. Two hundred years before, when the government of the Union had been transferred from Washington to Centropolis, the newspaper had followed the government — if it were not that the government had followed the newspaper — and it had taken its new title, the *Earth Herald*.

And let nobody imagine that it had declined under the administration of Francis Bennett. No! On the contrary, its new director had given it an equalled vitality and driving-power by the inauguration of telephonic journalism.

The inexplicable aerial phenomena which capture the public attention at the beginning of *Robur le Conquérant*.

Everybody knows that system, made possible by the incredible diffusion of the telephone. Every morning, instead of being printed as in antiquity, the *Earth Herald* is 'spoken'. It is by means of a brisk conversation with a reporter, a political figure, or a scientist, that the subscribers can learn whatever happens to interest them. As for those who buy an odd number for a few cents, they know that they can get acquainted with the day's issue through the countless phonographic cabinets.

This innovation of Francis Bennett restored new life to the old journal. In a few months its clientèle numbered eighty-five million subscribers, and the director's fortune rose to three hundred million dollars, and has since gone far beyond that. Thanks to this fortune, he was able to build his new office — a colossal edifice with four façades each two miles long, whose roof is sheltered beneath the glorious flag, with its seventy-five stars, of the Confederation.

Francis Bennett, king of journalists, would then have been king of the two Americas, if the Americans would ever accept any monarch whatever. Do you doubt this? But the plenipotentiaries of every nation and our very ministers, throng around his door, peddling their advice, seeking his approval, imploring the support of his all-powerful organ. Count up the scientists whom he has encouraged, the artists whom he em-

The airscrews which drive Robur's flying machine, the *Albatross*, and foreshadowed the modern helicopter.

ploys, the inventors whom he subsidises! A wearisome monarchy was his, work without respite, and certainly nobody of earlier times would ever have been able to carry out so unremitting a daily grind. Fortunately however, the men of today have a more robust constitution, thanks to the progress of hygiene and of gymnastics, which from thirty-seven years has now increased to sixty-eight the average length of human life — thanks too to the aseptic foods, while we wait for the next discovery: that of nutritious air which will enable us to take nourishment . . . only by breathing.

And now, if you would like to know everything that constitutes the day of a director of the *Earth Herald*, take the trouble to follow him in his multifarious operations — this very day, this July 25th of the present year, 2889.

That morning Francis Bennett awoke in rather a bad temper. This was eight days since his wife had been in France and he was feeling a little lonely. Can it be credited? They had been married ten years, and this was the first time that Mrs Edith Bennett, that *professional beauty*, had been so long away. Two or three days usually sufficed for her frequent journeys to Europe and especially Paris, where she went to buy her hats.

As soon as he awoke, Francis Bennett switched on his phonotelephote, whose wires led to the house he owned in the Champs-Elysées.

The telephone, completed by the telephote, is another of our time's conquests! Though the transmission of speech by the electric current was already very old, it was only since yesterday that vision could also be transmitted. A valuable discovery, and Francis Bennett was by no means the only one to bless its inventor when, in spite of the enormous distance between them, he saw his wife appear in the telephotic mirror.

The *Albatross* hovers over Paris bringing
the same touch of menace as the German
bombers of World War II.

A lovely vision! A little tired by last night's theatre or dance, Mrs Bennett was still in bed. Although where she was it was nearly noon, her charming head was buried in the lace of the pillow. But there she was stirring . . . her lips were moving . . . No doubt she was dreaming? . . . Yes! She was dreaming . . . A name slipped from her mouth. 'Francis . . . dear Francis! . . .'

His name, spoken by that sweet voice, gave a happier turn to Francis Bennett's mood. Not wanting to wake the pretty sleeper, he quickly jumped out of bed, and went into his mechanised dressing-room.

Two minutes later, without needing the help of a valet, the machine deposited him, washed, shaved, shod, dressed and buttoned from top to toe, on the threshold of his office. The day's work was going to begin.

It was into the room of the serialised novelists that Francis first entered.

Very big that room, surmounted by a large translucent dome. In a corner, several telephonic instruments by which the hundred authors of the *Earth Herald* related a hundred chapters of a hundred romances to the enfevered public.

Catching sight of one of these serialists who was snatching five minutes' rest, Francis Bennett said:

'Very fine, my dear fellow, very fine, that last chapter of yours! That scene where the young village girl is discussing with her admirer some of the problems of transcendental philosophy shows very keen powers of observation! These country manners have never been more clearly depicted! Go on that way, my dear Archibald, and good luck to you. Ten thousand new subscribers since yesterday, thanks to you!'

'Mr. John Last,' he continued, turning towards another of his collaborators, 'I'm not so satisfied with you! It hasn't any life, your story! You're in too much of a hurry to get to the end!

Aerial observation of a city as provided by the *Albatross* – a technique later developed to deadly effect.

Well! and what about all that documentation? You've got to dissect, John Last, you've got to dissect! It isn't with a pen one writes nowadays, it's with a scalpel! Every action in real life is the resultant of a succession of fleeting thoughts, and they've got to be carefully set out to create a living being! And what's easier than to use electrical hypnotism, which redoubles its subject and separates his two-fold personality! Watch yourself living, John Last, my dear fellow! Imitate your colleague whom I've just been congratulating! Get yourself hypnotised . . . What? . . . You're having it done, you say? . . . Not good enough yet, not good enough!'

Having given this little lesson, Francis Bennett continued his inspection and went on into the reporters' room. His fifteen hundred reporters, placed before an equal number of telephones, were passing on to subscribers the news which had come in during the night from the four quarters of the earth.

The organisation of this incomparable service has often been described. In addition to his telephone, each reporter has in front of him a series of commutators, which allow him to get into communication with this or that telephotic line. Thus the subscribers have not only the story but the sight of these events. When it is a question of 'miscellaneous facts', which are things of the past by the time they are described, their principal phases alone are transmitted; these are obtained by intensive photography.

The *Albatross* rains destruction on a helpless population – again foreshadowing a development in modern warfare.

Francis Bennett questioned one of the ten astronomical reporters – a service which was growing because of the recent discoveries in the stellar world.

'Well, Cash, what have you got?'

'Phototelegrams from Mercury, Venus and Mars, sir.'

'Interesting, that last one?'

'Yes! a revolution in the Central Empire, in support of the reactionary liberals against the republican conservatives.'

'Just like us, then! – And Jupiter?'

'Nothing so far! We haven't been able to understand the signals the Jovians make. Perhaps ours haven't reached them? . . .'

'That's your job, and I hold you responsible, Mr Cash!' Francis Bennett replied; extremely dissatisfied, he went on to the scientific editorial room.

Bent over their computers, thirty savants were absorbed in equations of the ninety-fifth degree. Some indeed were revelling in the formulae of algebraical infinity and of twenty-four dimensional space, like a child in the elementary class dealing with the four rules of arithmetic.

Francis Bennet fell among them rather like a bombshell.

'Well, gentlemen, what's this they tell me? No reply from Jupiter? . . . It's always the same! Look here, Corley, it seems to me its been twenty years that you've been pegging away at that planet . . .'

'What do you expect, sir?' the savant replied. 'Our optical science still leaves something to be desired, and even with our telescopes two miles long . . .'

'You hear that, Peer?' broke in Francis Bennett, addressing himself to Corley's neighbour. 'Optical science leaves something to be desired! . . . That's your speciality, that is, my dear fellow! Put on your glasses, devil take it! Put on your glasses!'

Then, turning back to Corley:

'But, failing Jupiter, aren't you getting some results from the moon, at any rate?'

'Not yet, Mr Bennett.'

'Well, this time, you can't blame optical science! The moon is six hundred times nearer than Mars, and yet our correspondence service is in

Mechanics performing an aerial repair job
on the *Albatross* to limit the chances of a
surprise attack.

regular operation with Mars. It can't be telescopes we're needing . . .'

'No, it's the inhabitants,' Corley replied with the thin smile of a savant stuffed with X.

'You dare tell me that the moon is uninhabited?'

'On the face it turns towards us, at any rate, Mr Bennett. Who knows whether on the other side?' . . .

'Well, there's a very simple method of finding out . . .' '

'And that is? . . .'

'To turn the moon round!'

And that very day, the scientists of the Bennett factory started working out some mechanical means of turning our satellite right round.

Two prisoners of the *Albatross* slip away under the cover of darkness – but the exploits of Robur are not finished yet . . .

On the whole Francis Bennett had reason to be satisfied. One of the *Earth Herald's* astronomers had just determined the elements of a new planet Gandini. It is at a distance of 12,841,348,284,623 meters and 7 decimeters that this planet describes its orbit round the sun in 572 years, 194 days, 12 hours, 43 minutes, 9.8 seconds.

Francis Bennet was delighted with such precision.

'Good!' he exclaimed, 'hurry up and tell the reportage service about it. You know what a passion the public has for these astronomical questions. I'm anxious for the news to appear in today's issue!'

Before leaving the reporters' room he took up another matter with a special group of interviewers, addressing the one who dealt with celebrities: 'You've interviewed President Wilcox?' he asked.

'Yes, Mr Bennett, and I'm publishing the information that he's certainly suffering from a dilatation of the stomach, and that he's most conscientiously undergoing a course of tubular irrigations.'

'Splendid. And that business of Chapmann the assassin? . . . Have you interviewed the jurymen who are to sit at the Assizes?'

'Yes, and they all agree that he's guilty, so that the case won't even have to be submitted to them. The accused will be executed before he's sentenced.'

'Splendid! Splendid!'

The next room, a broad gallery about a quarter of a mile long, was devoted to publicity, and it well may be imagined what the publicity for such a journal as the *Earth Herald* had to be. It brought in a daily average of three million dollars. Very ingeniously, indeed, some of the publicity obtained took an absolutely novel form, the result of a patent bought at an outlay of three dollars from a poor devil who had since died of hunger. They are gigantic signs reflected on the clouds, so large that they can be seen all over a whole country. From that gallery a thousand projectors were unceasingly employed in sending to the clouds, on which they were reproduced in colour,

A mystery machine capable of enormous speeds on land, in the sea or in the air terrifies the population: an opening scene from *The Master of the World*.

these inordinate advertisements.

But that day when Francis Bennett entered the publicity room he found the technicians with their arms folded beside their idle projectors. He asked them about it . . . The only reply he got was that somebody pointed to the blue sky.

'Yes! . . . A fine day,' he muttered, 'so we can't get any aerial publicity! What's to be done about that? If there isn't any rain, we can produce it! But it isn't rain, it's clouds that we need!'

'Yes, some fine snow-white clouds!' replied the chief technician.

'Well, Mr Simon Mark, you'd better get in touch with the scientific editors' meteorological service. You can tell them from me that they can get busy on the problem of artificial clouds. We really can't be at the mercy of the fine weather.'

After finishing his inspection of the different sections of the paper, Francis Bennett went to his reception hall, where he found awaiting him the ambassadours and plenipotentiary ministers accredited to the American government: these gentlemen had come to ask advice from the all-powerful director. As he entered the room they were carrying on rather a lively discussion.

'Pardon me, your Excellency', the French Ambassador addressed the Ambassador from Russia. 'But I can't see anything that needs changing in the map of Europe. The north to the Slavs, agreed! But the south to the Latins! Our common frontier along the Rhine seems quite satisfactory. Understand me clearly, that our government will certainly resist any attempt which may be made against our Prefectures of Rome, Madrid, and Vienna!'

'Well said!' Francis Bennett intervened in the discussion. 'What Mr Russian Ambassador, you're not satisfied with you great empire, which extends from the banks of the Rhine as far as the frontiers of China? An empire whose immense coast is bathed by the Arctic Ocean, the Atlantic, the Black Sea, the Bosphorus, and the Indian Ocean?

'And besides, what's the use of threats? Is war with our modern weapons possible? These asphyxiating shells which can be sent a distance of a hundred miles, these electric flashes, sixty miles long, which can annihilate a whole army corps at a single blow, these projectiles loaded with the microbes of plague, cholera, and yellow fever, and which can destroy a whole nation in a few hours?'

'We realise that, Mr Bennett,' the Russian Ambassador replied. 'But are

Excited crowds everywhere gathering to read news of the mystery machine and its incredible feats.

we free to do what we like? . . . Thrust back ourselves by the Chinese on our Eastern frontier, we must, at all costs, attempt something towards the west . . .'

'Is that all it is, sir?' Francis Bennett replied in reassuring tones — 'Well! as the proliferation of the Chinese is getting to be a danger to the world, we'll bring pressure to bear on the Son of Heaven. He'll simply have to impose a maximum birth-rate on his subjects, not to be exceeded on pain of death! A child too many? . . . A father less! That will keep things balanced.

'And you, Sir,' the director of the *Earth Herald* continued, addressing the English consul, 'what can I do to be of service to you?'

'A great deal, Mr Bennett,' that personage replied. 'It would be enough for your journal to open a campaign on our behalf . . .'

'And with what purpose?'

'Merely to protest against the annexation of Great Britain by the United States . . .'

'Merely that!' Francis Bennett exclaimed. He shrugged his shoulders. 'An annexation that's a hundred and fifty years old already! But won't you English gentry ever resign yourselves to the fact that by a just compensation of events here below, their country has become an American colony? That's pure madness! How could you government ever have believed that I should ever open so antipatriotic a compaign . . .'

'Mr Bennett, you know that the Monroe doctrine is all America for the Americans, and nothing more than America, and not . . .'

'But England is only one of our colonies, one of the finest. Don't count upon our ever consenting to give her up!'

'You refuse?' . . .

'I refuse, and if you insist, we shall make it a *casus belli*, based on nothing more than an interview with one of our reporters.'

'So that's the end,' the consul was overwhelmed. 'The United Kingdon, Canada, and New Britain belong to the Americans, India to the Russians, and Australia and New Zealand to themselves! Of all that once was England, what's left? . . . Nothing!'

'Nothing, Sir?' retorted Francis Bennett. 'Well, what about Gibraltar?'

At that moment the clock struck twelve. The director of the *Earth Herald*, ending the audience with a gesture, left the hall, and sat down in a rolling armchair. In a few minutes he had reached his dining room, half a mile away, at the far end of the office.

The table was laid, and he took his place at it. Within reach of his hand was placed a series of taps, and before him was the curved surface of a phonotelephote, on which appeared the dining-room of his home in Paris. Mr and Mrs Bennett had arranged to have lunch at the same time — nothing could be more pleasant than to be face to face in spite of the distance, to see one another and talk by means of the phototelephotic apparatus.

But the room in Paris was still empty.

The secret revealed: a first glimpse of the all-purpose machine, the *Terrible*, in the sky.

'Edith is late,' Francis Bennett said to himself. 'Oh, women's punctuality! Everything makes progress, except that.'

And after this too just reflection, he turned on one of the taps.

Like everybody else in easy circumstances nowadays, Francis Bennett, having abandoned domestic cooking, is one of the subscribers to the *Society*

The *Terrible* lands in its secret hideout in the heart of America in the Great Eyry.

for *Supplying Food to the Home*, which distributes dishes of a thousand types through a network of pneumatic tubes. This system is expensive, no doubt, but the cooking is better, and it has the advantage that it has suppressed that hair-raising race, the cooks of both sexes.

So, not without some regret, Francis Bennett was lunching in solitude. He was finishing his coffee when Mrs Bennett, having got back home, appeared in the telephoto screen.

'Where have you been, Edith dear?' Francis Bennett enquired.

'What?' Mrs Bennett replied. 'You've finished? . . . I must be late, then? . . . Where have I been? Of course, I've been with my *modiste* . . . This year's hats are so bewitching! They're not hats at all . . . they're domes, they're cupolas! I rather lost count of time!'

'Rather, my dear? You lost it so much that here's my lunch finished.'

'Well, run along then, my dear . . . run along to your work,' Mrs Bennett replied. 'I've still got a visit to make, to my *modeleur-couturier.*'

And this *couturier* was no other than the famous Wormspire, the very man who so judiciously remarked 'Woman is only a question of shape!'

Francis Bennett kissed Mrs Bennett's cheek on the telephote screen and went across to the window, where his aerocar was waiting.

'Where are we going, Sir?' asked the aero-coachman.

'Let's see. I've got time . . .' Francis Bennett replied. 'Take me to my accumulator works at Niagara.'

The aero-car, an apparatus splendidly based on the principle of 'heavier than air', shot across space at a speed of about four hundred miles an hour. Below him were spread out the towns with their moving pavements which carry the wayfarers along the streets, and the countryside, covered, as though by an immense spider's web, by the network of electric wires.

Within half-an-hour, Francis Bennett had reached his works at Niagara, where, after using the force of the cataracts to produce energy, he sold or hired it out to the consumers. Then, his visit over, he returned, by way of Philadelphia, Boston, and New

Robur again! The conqueror shows himself once more – at the wheel of his masterful new creation.

York, to Centropolis, where his aerocar put him down about five o'clock.

The waiting room of the *Earth Herald* was crowded. A careful look-out was being kept for Francis Bennett to return for the daily audience he gave to his petitioners. They included the capital's acquisitive inventors, company promotors with enterprises to suggest — all splendid, to listen to them. Among these different proposals he had to make a choice, reject the bad ones, look into the doubtful ones, give a welcome to the good ones.

He soon got rid of those who had only got useless or impracticable schemes. One of them — didn't he claim to revive painting, an art which had fallen into such destitution that Millet's *Angelus* had just been sold for fifteen francs — thanks to the progress of colour photography invented at the end of the twentieth century by the Japanese, whose name was on everybody's lips — Aruziswa-Riochi-Nichome-Sanjukamboz-Kio-Baski-Kû? Another, hadn't he discovered the biogene bacillus which, after being introduced into the human organism, would make man immortal? This one, a chemist, hadn't he discovered a new substance. *Nihilium*, of which a gram would cost only three million dollars? That one, a most daring physician, wasn't he claiming that he'd found a remedy for a cold in the head?

All these dreamers were at once shown out.

A few of the others received a better welcome, and foremost among them was a young man whose broad brow indicated a high degree of intelligence.

'Sir,' he began, 'though the number of elements used to be estimated at seventy-five, it has now been reduced to three, as no doubt you are aware?'

'Perfectly,' Francis Bennett replied.

'Well, sir, I'm on the point of reducing the three to one. If I don't run out of money I'll have succeeded in three weeks.'

'And then?'

'Then, sir, I shall really have discovered the absolute.'

'And the results of that discovery?'

'It will be to make the creation of all forms of matter easy — stone, wood, metal, fibrin . . .'

'Are you saying you're going to be able to construct a human being?'

'Completely . . . The only thing missing will be the soul!'

'Only that!' was the ironical reply of Francis Bennett, who however assigned the young fellow to the scientific editorial department of his journal.

A second inventor, using as a basis some old experiments that dated from the nineteeth century and had often been repeated since, had the idea of moving a whole city in a single block. He suggested, as a demonstration, the town of Saaf, situated fifteen miles from the sea; after conveying it on rails down to the shore, he would transform it into a seaside resort. That would add an enormous value to the ground already built on and to be built over.

Francis Bennett, attracted by this project, agreed to take a half share in it.

'You know, sir,' said a third applicant, 'that, thanks to our solar and terrestrial accumulators and transformers, we've been able to equalise the seasons. I suggest doing even better. By converting into heat part of the energy we have at our disposal and transmitting the head to the polar regions we can melt the ice . . .'

'Leave your plans with me,' Francis Bennett replied, 'and come back in a week.'

The *Terrible* having been chased on land is now pursued by destroyers at sea.

The end for the great Robur and his machine, the *Terrible,* in a fearful electrical explosion.

Finally, a fourth savant brought the news that one of the questions which had excited the whole world was about to be solved that very evening.

As is well known, a century ago a daring experiment made by Dr Nathaniel Faithburn had attracted public attention. A convinced supporter of the idea of human hibernation — the possibility of arresting the vital functions and then reawakening them after a certain time — he had decided to test the value of the method on himself. After, by a holograph will, describing the operations necessary to restore him to life a hundred years later to the day, he had exposed himself to a cold of 172° centigrade (278° fahrenheit) below zero; thus reduced to a mummified state, he had been shut up in a tomb for the stated period.

Just one of the many successful reprints of *The Master of the World* in *Amazing Stories*, February 1928. The illustration is by Frank Paul.

Now it was exactly on that very day, July, 2889, that the period expired, and Francis Bennett had just received an offer to proceed in one of the rooms of the *Earth Herald* office with the resurrection so impatiently waited for.

The public could then be kept in touch with it second by second.

The proposal was accepted, and as the operation was not to take place until ten that evening, Francis Bennett went to stretch himself out in an easy chair in the audition room. Then, pressing a button, he was put into communication with the Central Concert.

After so busy a day, what a charm he found in the works of our greatest masters, based, as everybody knows, on a series of delicious harmonico-algebraic formulae!

The room had been darkened, and, plunged into an ecstatic half-sleep, Francis Bennett could not even see himself. But a door opened suddenly.

'Who's there?' he asked, touching a commutator placed beneath his hand.

At once, by an electric effect produced on the ether, the air became luminous.

'Oh, it's you, doctor?' he asked.

'Myself' replied Dr Sam, who had come to pay his daily visit (annual subscription). 'How's it going?'

'Fine!'

'All the better ... Let's see your tongue?'

He looked at it through a microscope.

'Good ... And your pulse?'

He tested it with a pulsograph, similar to the instruments which record earthquakes.

'Splendid! ... And you appetite?'

'Ugh!'

'Oh, your stomach! ... It isn't going too well, your stomach! ... It's getting old, your stomach is! ... We'll certainly have to get you a new one!'

'We'll see!' Francis Bennett replied, 'and meantime, doctor, you'll dine with me.'

During the meal, phonotelephotic communication had been set up with Paris. Mrs Bennett was at her table this time, and the dinner, livened up by Dr Sam's jokes, was delightful. Hardly was it over than:

Vincent Price brings Robur to the screen in
the 1961 film of *Master of the World.*

The latest version of *Master of the World* produced by Marvel Comics with illustrations by Dino Castrillo (1977).

'When do you expect to get back to Centropolis, dear Edith?' asked Francis Bennett.

'I'm going to start this moment.'

'By tube or aero-train?' 'By tube.'

'Then you'll be here?'

'At eleven fifty-nine this evening.'

'Paris time?'

'No, no! . . . Centropolis time.'

'Good-bye then, and above all don't miss the tube!'

These submarine tubes, by which one travels from Paris in two hundred and ninety-five minutes, are certainly much preferable to the aero-trains, which only manage six hundred miles an hour.

The doctor had gone, after promising to return to be present at the resurrection of his colleague Nathaniel Faithburn. Wishing to draw up his daily accounts, Francis Bennett went into his private office. An enormous operation, when it concerns an enterprise whose expenditure rises to eight hundred thousand dollars every day! Fortunately, the development of modern mechanisation has greatly facilitated this work. Helped by the piano-electric-computor, Francis Bennett soon completed his task.

It was time. Hardly had he struck the last key of the mechanical totalisator than his presence was asked for in the experimental room. He went off to it at once, and was welcomed by a large cortège of scientists, who had been joined by Dr Sam.

Nathaniel Faithburn's body is there, on the bier, placed on trestles in the centre of the room.

The telephoto is switched on. The whole world will be able to follow the various phases of the operation.

The coffin is opened . . . Nathaniel Faithburn's body is taken out . . . It is still like a mummy, yellow, hard, dry. It sounds like wood . . . It is submitted to heat . . . electricity . . . No result . . . It's hypnotised . . . It's exposed to suggestion . . . Nothing can overcome that ultra-cataleptic state.

'Well, Dr Sam?' asks Francis Bennett.

Jules Verne

The doctor leans over the body; he examines it very carefully . . . He introduces into it, by means of an hypodermic, a few drops of the famous Brown-Séquard elixir, which is once again in fashion . . . The mummy is more mummified than ever.

'Oh well' Dr Sam replies 'I think the hibernation has lasted too long . . .'

'Oh!'

'And Nathaniel Faithburn is dead.'

'Dead?'

'As dead as anybody could be!'

'And how long has he been dead?'

'How long?' . . . Dr Sam replies. 'But . . . a hundred years — that is to say, since he had the unhappy idea of freezing himself for pure love of science!'

'Then,' Francis Bennett comments, 'that's a method which still needs to be perfected!'

'Perfected is the word,' replies Dr Sam, while the scientific commission on hibernation carries away its funereal bundle.

* * *

Followed by Dr Sam, Francis Bennett regained his room, and as he seemed very tired after so very full a day, the doctor advised him to take a bath before going to bed.

'You're quite right, doctor . . . That will refresh me . . .'

'It will, Mr Bennett, and if you like I'll order one on my way out . . .'

'There's no need for that, doctor. There's always a bath all ready in the office, and I needn't even have the trouble of going out of my room to take it. Look, simply by touching this button, that bath will start moving, and you'll see it come along all by itself with the water at a temperature of sixty-five degrees!'

Francis Bennett had just touched the button. A rumbling sound began, got louder, increased . . . Then one of the doors opened, and the bath appeared, gliding along on its rails . . .

Heavens! While Dr Sam veils his face, little screams of frightened modesty arise from the bath . . .

Brought to the office by the transatlantic tube half an hour before, Mrs Bennett was inside it!

* * *

Next day, July 26, 2889, the director of the *Earth Herald* recommenced his tour of twelve miles across his office. That evening, when his totalisator had been brought into action, it was at two hundred and fifty thousand dollars that it calculated the profits of that day — fifty thousand more than the day before.

A fine job, that of a journalist at the end of the twenty-ninth century!

One of the first foreign writers to exploit the same vein of scientific adventure as Jules Verne was the American Luis Senarens who created Frank Reade, a boy genius who invented aeroplanes, helicopters, submarines, robots and super land machines of all shapes and sizes. These remarkable weekly stories earned Senarens the title 'The American Jules Verne' and his publishers were not above claiming that he had even outdone the French grandmaster of imagination! These are typical titles from almost two hundred he wrote about Frank Reade between 1880 and 1892.

Frank Reade's Air Ship which featured in the adventures by Luis Senarens was similar to Verne's *Albatross* in both capability and power.

Though Verne lived much of his life as a recluse in Amiens, he could be tempted away occasionally, and when he was 62, he actually agreed to go on a short balloon ascent! This event in 1890 was part of a plan to get support for a proposed balloon crossing of the Atlantic — a feat that still remains to be achieved today.

A JULES VERNE BIBLIOGRAPHY

Les Voyages Extraordinaires

Five Weeks in a Balloon (1863)
Journey to the Centre of the Earth (1864)
From the Earth to the Moon (1865)
The Adventures of Captain Hatteras (2 Vols: 1866)
The Children of Captain Grant (3 Vols: 1868)
Round the Moon (1870)
Twenty Thousand Leagues Under the Sea (1870)
A Floating City (1871)
Adventures of Three Russians & Three Englishmen (1872)
Around the World in Eighty Days (1873)
The Fur Country (2 Vols: 1873)
Doctor Ox's Experiment (1874)
The Mysterious Island (3 Vols: 1875)
The Survivors of 'The Chancellor' (1875)
Michael Strogoff (2 Vols: 1876)
Child of the Cavern (1877)
Hector Servadac (2 Vols: 1877)

Jules Verne described his *Hector Servadac* (1877) as 'more fantastic than *From the Earth to the Moon*' and told his publisher that it was 'a lot of fantasy mixed with a great deal of serious science'. It is basically the story of a trip around the solar system, but there is less of the probable in it than most of his other works and perhaps he indicated this with the macabre pun in the title. Just reverse Hector's surname . . .

Dick Sands, The Boy Captain (1878)
The Begum's Fortune (1879)
The Tribulations of a Chinese
 Gentleman (1879)
The Steam House (2 Vols: 1880)
The Giant Raft (2 Vols: 1881)
The School for Crusoes (1882)
The Green Ray (1882)
Kereban the Inflexible (2 Vols: 1883)
The Southern Star Mystery (1884)
The Archipelago on Fire (1884)
Mathias Sandorf (2 Vols: 1885)
Salvage from the 'Cynthia' (with
 André Laurie, 1885)
The Clipper of the Clouds (1886)
The Lottery Ticket (1886)
North Against South (2 Vols: 1887)
The Flight to France (1887)
Two Years' Holiday (2 Vols: 1888)
The Purchase of the North Pole
 (1889)
A Family Without A Name (1889)
Cesar Cascabel (2 Vols: 1890)
Mistress Branican (2 Vols: 1891)
The Carpathian Castle (1892)
Claudius Bombarnac (1893)
Foundling Mick (2 Vols: 1893)
The Adventures of Captain Antifer (2
 Vols: 1894)
Propeller Island (2 Vols: 1895)
For The Flag (1896)
Clovis Dardentor (1896)
The Sphinx of the Icefields (2 Vols:
 1897)

The Barsac Mission (1920) which Verne
left uncompleted at his death and was
finished by his son described an 'ideal city'
created in the heart of the Sahara Desert,
and anticipated modern broadcasting.
(*Below*) *Deux Ans de Vacances* (1888)
another of Verne's 'Robinsonnades' deals
with a group of New Zealand schoolchildren shipwrecked on a desert island and
how two boys, one French and the other
English, enable the group to overcome all
manner of difficulties before their final
rescue.

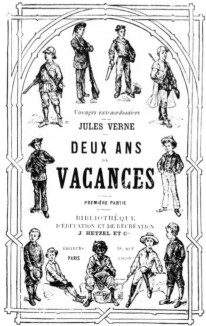

Le Superbe Orénoque (No translation: 1898)

The Testament of an Eccentric (2 Vols: 1899)

Second Fatherland (2 Vols: 1900)

The Aerial Village (1901)

Les Histoires de Jean-Marie Cabidoulin (No translation: 1901)

Les Frères Kip (2 Vols; No translation: 1902)

Bourses de Voyage (2 Vols; No translation: 1903)

Master of the World (1904)

Un Drame en Livonie (No translation: 1904)

L'Invasion de la Mer (No translation: 1905)

The Lighthouse at the End of the World (1905)

The Golden Volcano (2 Vols: 1906)

The Thompson Travel Agency (2 Vols: 1907)

The Chase of the Golden Meteor (1908)

Le Pilote du Danube (No translation: 1908)

The 'Jonathan' (3 Vols: 1909)

The Secret of Wilhelm Storitz (1910)

Hier et Demain (short stories: 1910)

The Barsac Mission (2 Vols: 1920)

(*Right*) The floating ice island which shrinks from 150 square miles to the size of a raft before a scientific genius manages to stop the melting by freezing the flow in *The Fur Country* (1873).

Jules Verne was a great nationalist and several times espoused the causes of those fighting for their country in the face of tyranny and despotism. Two examples of this are (*opposite*) *Martin Paz* one of his earliest stories about a revolt in Lima (1852); and (*above*) *Flight to France* in which a young man born in Prussia of French parents is called up to serve against France, but deserts to join his true countrymen at the crucial moment (1887).

The continuing popularity of Verne shown in a school primer of *Journey to the Centre of the Earth* (Pendulum Press, 1974); Marvel Comics picture strip version of *The Mysterious Island* with illustrations by E. R. Cruz (1976) and the Panther Books paperback edition of *The Secret of Wilhelm Storitz* (1965). The last named has been compared to H. G. Wells' *The Invisible Man* as it also deals with the possibilities of invisibility.

Verne's name is today rarely out of the newspapers for long as one after another of his prophecies come true. And there is every indication that this will continue far into the future. . . . The advertisement was from *The Sunday Times* June 4, 1974.

Jules Verne, you were nearer the truth than we thought!

Two thirds of the earth's surface is water. Below it lie vast mineral wealth and sources of food. The undersea world of hydrospace.

With its unrivalled experience and expertise in underwater cable and communications systems, STC is an undisputed leader in the growing technologies necessary for the exploitation of this underwater world. STC provides complete undersea cable systems for many marine activities, including subsea oil wellheads, diving, submersibles, maritime survey, as well as glands and cable handling equipment.

The future with STC. As a world leader in the field of communications, STC is mindful of its responsibilities to the men and women on

whose skills and creativity the future depends. STC practises an open and flexible style of management; and it has evolved a well-defined personnel policy, including training and career development, to enable staff to benefit from new techniques and technologies and to fulfill their potential within the Company.

If you're at the start of your career or an experienced engineer looking for further scope, watch out for vacancies in individual advertisements – or to learn more about STC and what we can offer you, write for our Information Pack to: Juliet Rowe (Ref. SF), Personnel Department, Standard Telephones and Cables Limited, STC House, 190 Strand, London WC2R 1DU.

STC Changing the face of communications worldwide

Is science fiction a new religion for the young?

DO YOU believe in life on other planets? If you're under 40 your answer is almost certainly yes

INTRODUCING THE STRANGE STORY OF THREE OBSESSED PEOPLE

The quiet man behind that Verne comeback

Jules Verne : Science fiction factory.

Magic carpets
by RICHARD LANE

JULES VERNE by Jean Jules-Verne translated and adapted by Roger Greaves (Macdonald & Jane's £6.50)

THE child's discovery of fantasy is like being given a box of supernatural

THIS is a story of obsession; the tale of three obsessed men. Each has a part in a strange and terrifying new book which is about to be published.

One, an American, is already secure in literary esteem. The second, a Frenchman, may soon be regaining the vast fame he once possessed. The third, from Britain, is virtually unknown.

LET US LOOK AT THE AMERICAN FIRST.

The world last saw him as he lay in torment after years of drug-taking. His hands clawed at his parched throat. He kept crying to be rescued from the ship's hold. "Save me, save poor Pym," he

Advice from Jules Verne...

THE subtitle of Erich von Däniken's ACCORDING TO THE EVIDENCE (Souvenir Press, £4·50) is My proof of Man's Extra-terrestrial Origins, which sounds challenging enough. But throughout the book von Däniken is uncharacteristically on the defensive; indeed he places himself, as it were, in the dock of some Supreme Court, the brave original thinker taking on a pack of unimaginative critics who remain unimpressed by such "evidence" as a 3000-year-old Colombian figurine

Däniken with Chariots of the Gods? and its successors (38 million say his happy publishers) or his capacity for beavering away at his pet subject—typically Swiss, you might say, as is the paucity of humour in his writing, unless you count such unconsciously funny passages as his chat with Jules Verne, who died in 1905 ("a leading medium successeded in putting me in phonic communication . . ," which the Frenchman advised von Däniken, when making forecasts, to "proceed on realistic assumptions."

Better still, perhaps should try his luck at science fiction . . .

Richard Bruto

BEST SELLERS
THE Country

ACKNOWLEDGEMENTS

This book would not have been possible without the help of one man in particular, I. O. Evans, whose knowledge and love for the works of Jules Verne has done much to popularise him among English-speaking readers. He was always generous with advice and not only secured several of the very rare Verne items which appear in this book for the first time, but also made the translations with enthusiasm and care. It is to my great sorrow that he died before he could see the fruits of his efforts in finished form. I should also like to thank the following who contributed in various ways: *The New Statesman*, Times Newspapers, The British Museum Newspaper Library, The London Library, *La Monde*, *The Spectator*, Souvenir Press Ltd, Marvel Comics Inc., Pendulum Press Inc., Panther Books, British Film Institute, M.G.M. Pictures, Columbia Pictures and Walt Disney Inc.